Victory & Self-Mastery

VICTORY and SELF-MASTERY

Through an

Understanding of the

Son of God in His Humanity —

The Pattern Man

by

J. H N. TINDALL

"The **humanity of the Son of God** is everything to us. It is the **golden chain** that binds our souls to Christ, and through Christ to God. **This is to be our study.** Christ was a real man; He gave proof of His humility by becoming a man. Yet He was God in the flesh. When we approach this subject, we would do well to heed the words spoken by Christ to Moses at the burning bush, 'Put off thy shoes from off thy feet, for the place whereon thou standest is holy ground.' We should come to this study with the humility of a learner, with a contrite heart. And the study of the incarnation of Christ is a **fruitful field,** which will repay the searcher who digs for hidden truth." — **Youth's Instructor,** Oct. 13, 1898. (QOD 647).

TEACH Services, Inc.
New York

2004   05   06   07   08   09   10   11   12   · 5   4   3   2   1

Copyright © 1993, 2004 TEACH Services, Inc.
ISBN 1-57258-256-0
Library of Congress Catalog Card No. 2003112797

Published by
TEACH Services, Inc.
www.TEACHServices.com

CONTENTS

INTRODUCTION

Elder John Tindall styled himself a "converted athiest." After two years of training at Loma Linda, 1908-1910, he finished the Medical Evangelist Course and went out as the first graduate to conduct gospel medical missionary evangelism. Throughout his more than fifty years of promoting this divine method of soul winning he ever upheld Christ as the perfect example of what all His believers are to become in character.

This book primarily presents Christ in His humanity, which Sister White declares is "everything to us." Being a compilation of several studies, it is understandable why some quotations are repeated several times. As he ever continued studying this glorious truth, and as advanced light came to him, he revised his work to conform to that light. Those who have his former editions will note that this edition gives a greatly enlarged coverage of the topic and that some revisions have been made.

I

MAN AND MIND THE CROWNING ACT
OF THE CREATION OF GOD

SD 7 (RH Feb. 11, 1902): "God created man a **superior being;** he alone is formed in the image of God, and is capable of partaking of the divine nature, of cooperating with his Creator and executing His plans."

2SM 252 (ST June 9, 1898): "After the fall of man, Satan declared that human beings were proved to be incapable of keeping the law of God, and he sought to carry the universe with him in this belief. Satan's words appeared to be true, and Christ came to unmask the deceiver. The Majesty of Heaven undertook the cause of man, and with the same facilities that man may obtain, withstood the temptations of Satan as man must withstand them. This was the only way in which fallen man could become a partaker of the divine nature."

DA 671: "Through the Spirit the believer becomes a partaker of the divine nature. Christ has given His Spirit as a divine power to overcome all hereditary and cultivated tendencies to evil, and to impress His own character upon His church."

RH June 18, 1895: "Man was the crowning act of the creation of God, made in the image of God, and **designed to be a counterpart of God** . . . " (Webster: or duplicate).

TM 170: "For ten days the disciples prayed before the Pentecostal blessing came. It required all that time to bring them to an understanding of what it meant to offer effectual prayer, drawing nearer and nearer to God, confessing their sins, humbling their hearts before God and by faith beholding Jesus and becoming changed into His image."

DA 478: "Christ came that He might recreate the image of God in man."

SD 28 (MS 28, 1886): "The redeemed will be given entrance into the royal family."

Bible Echo Jan. 1, 1888: "With the addition of this planet God finished His Creation work . . ."

1

RH June 25 1908: "Human beings . . . were a new and distinct order, made in the image of God."

ST May 31, 1896: "It was a wonderful thing for God to create man, **TO MAKE MIND. He created him that every faculty might be the faculty of His divine mind.** The glory of God is to be revealed in the creating of man in God's image, and in His redemption."

GC 474: "Every sinful gratification tends to benumb the faculties and deaden the mental and spiritual perceptions, and the word or the Spirit of God can make but a feeble impression upon the heart."

Ed 17: "Every human being, created in the image of God. is endowed with a power akin to that of the Creator—individuality, power to think and to do. — It is the work of true education to develop this power, to train the youth to be thinkers, and not mere reflectors of other men's thoughts."

FE 425-426: "We are God's workmanship, and His word declares that we are 'fearfully and wonderfully made.' **He has prepared this living habitation for the mind; it is** 'curiously wrought,' **a TEMPLE** which the Lord Himself has fitted up for the indwelling of the Holy Spirit."

DA 123: " 'The prince of this world cometh' said Jesus, 'and hath nothing in Me.' There was nothing in Him that responded to Satan's sophistry. He did not consent to sin. **Not even by a thought did He yield to temptation. So it may be with us.** Christ's humanity was united with divinity; **He was fitted for the conflict by the indwelling of the Holy Spirit.** And He came to make us partakers of the divine nature. So long as we are united to Him by faith, sin has no more dominion over us. God reaches for the hand of faith in us to direct it to lay fast hold upon the divinity of Christ, that we may attain to perfection of character."

5T 219: "His Spirit is a renewing power, transforming to the divine image all who will receive it."

7BC 926 (Letter 121, 1897): "That He might restore in man the original mind which he lost in Eden."

ST June 29, 1898: "Christ came to the earth, taking humanity and standing as man's representative, to show in the controversy with Satan, that man as God created him, **connected with the Father and the Son,** could obey every divine requirement."

2

THE SANCTUARY REVEALS THE PURPOSE
FOR THE HUMAN SOUL

Ed 36: "Through Christ was to be fulfilled the purpose of which the tabernacle was a symbol, — . . . In all, God desired His people to read **His purpose for the human soul.**"

IHP 154 (RH Jan. 11, 1912): "The Lord gave an important lesson to His people in all ages when to Moses on the mount He gave instruction regarding the building of the tabernacle. In that work He required perfection in every detail . . . Into all to which the Christian sets his hand should be woven the thought of the life eternal. If the work performed is agricultural or mechanical in its nature, it may still be after the pattern of the heavenly . . . "

RH Feb. 11, 1890: "Christ is cleansing the temple in heaven from the sins of the people, and we must work in harmony with Him upon the earth, cleansing the soul temple from its moral defilement."

DA 161: "From eternal ages it was God's purpose that **every created being** . . . should be a **temple for the indwelling of the Creator.**"

TM 47: "We cannot overestimate the importance of the union of divinity with humanity."

MH 180: "Christ came to make us partakers of the divine nature, and His word declares that humanity combined with divinity does not commit sin."

COL 320: "But Christ came in the form of humanity and by His perfect obedience He proved that humanity and divinity combined can obey every one of God's precepts."

THE FOUNTAIN OF LIFE REVEALED

DA 187: "He in whom Christ dwells, has within himself the fountain of blessing, — 'a well of water springing up into everlasting life.' "

Rev. 3:20: "Behold, I stand at the door, and knock; if any man hear my voice and open the door, I will come in to him, and will sup with him, and he with me."

Eph. 3:9-11: "And to make all men see what is the FELLOW-SHIP of the MYSTERY which from the beginning of the world hath been hid in God, who created all things by Jesus Christ: To the intent that now unto the principalities and powers in heavenly places might be known by the church the manifold wisdom of God, according to the eternal purpose which He purposed in Christ Jesus our Lord."

FILB 135 (RH Dec. 16, 1884): "The evil tendencies of mankind are hard to overcome. The battles are tedious. Every soul in the strife knows how severe, how bitter, are these contests. Everything about growth in grace is difficult, because the standard maxims of the world are constantly interposed between the soul and God's holy standard. . . . We must gain the victory over self, crucify the affections and lusts; and then begins the union of the soul with Christ . . . After this union is formed, it can be preserved only by continual, earnest, painstaking effort.

"Every Christian must stand on guard continually, watching every avenue of the soul, where Satan might find access. He must pray for divine help and at the same time resolutely resist every inclination to sin. By courage, by faith, by persevering toil, he can conquer. But let him remember that to gain the victory Christ must abide in him and he in Christ. . . . It is only by personal union with Christ, by communion with Him daily, hourly, that we can bear the fruits of the Holy Spirit."

Spl TM 47: "We cannot overestimate the importance of the union of divinity with humanity."

COL 320: "But Christ came in the form of humanity and by His perfect obedience He proved that humanity and divinity combined can obey every one of God's precepts."

8T 269: "The unity that exists between Christ and His disciples does not destroy the personality of either. They are one in purpose, in mind, in character, but not in person. It is thus that God and Christ are one."

1 Pet. 1:12: "Which things the angels desire to look into."

NO SHORT CUT TO HOLINESS

5T 500: "This is an age famous for surface work, for easy methods, for boasted holiness aside from the standard of character that God has erected. All short routes, all cutoff tracks, all teaching which fails to exalt the law of God as the standard of religious character, is spurious. Perfection of character is a lifelong work, unattainable by those who are not willing to strive for it in God's appointed way, by slow and toilsome steps. We cannot afford to make any mistake in this matter . . ."

FILB 217 (RH Oct. 5, 1886): "If an inquirer after salvation were to ask 'What must I do to inherit eternal life?' the modern teachers of salvation would answer, 'only believe that Jesus saves you . . . No value is attached to a mere profession of faith in Christ; only the love which is shown by works is counted genuine."

RH April 11, 1880: "The pleasing fable that all there is to do is to believe, has destroyed thousands and tens of thousands, because many have called that faith which is not faith, but simply a dogma. Man is an intelligent, accountable, being. He is not to be carried as a passive burden by the Lord, but is to work in harmony with Christ. Man is to take up his appointed work in striving for glory, honor and immortality. God calls upon man for the use of every talent He has lent them, the exercise of every power He has given them; for man can never be saved in disobedience and indolence."

2SM 381 (L 55, 1886): "I do not mean that cheap faith unsupported by works, but that earnest, living, constant, abiding faith, that eats the flesh and drinks the blood of the Son of God."

1SM 382 (ST June 16, 1896): "When it is in the heart to obey God, when efforts are put forth to this end, Jesus accepts this disposition and effort as man's best service, and He makes up for the deficiency with His own divine merit. But He will not accept those who claim to have faith in Him, and yet are disloyal to His Father's commandment. We hear a great deal about faith, but we need to hear a great deal more about works. Many are deceiving their own souls by living an easygoing accommodating, crossless religion. But Jesus says, "If any man will come after me, let him deny himself, and take up his cross, and follow me."

COL 331: "But Christ has given us no assurance that to attain perfection of character is an easy matter. A noble, all-round character is not inherited. It does not come to us by accident. A noble character is earned by individual effort through the merits and grace of Christ. God gives the talents, the powers of the mind; we form the character. It is formed by hard, stern battles with self. Conflict after conflict must be waged against hereditary tendencies. We shall have to criticize ourselves closely, and allow not one unfavorable trait to remain uncorrected."

IHP 47 (RH Dec. 21, 1886): "Character is not obtained by having others fight the battle of life for us. It must be sought, worked for, fought for, and it requires a purpose, a will, a determination. To form a character which God will approve, requires persevering effort. It will take a continual resisting of the powers of darkness to have our names retained in the book of life."

GC 472: "The desire for an easy religion that requires no striving, no self-denial, no divorce from the follies of the world, has made the doctrine of faith and faith only, a popular doctrine; but what saith the word of God? Says the apostle James: 'What doth it profit, my brethren, though a man say he hath faith, and have not works? Can faith save him? . . . will thou know, O vain man, that faith without works is dead? Was not Abraham our father justified by works, when he had offered Isaac, his son, upon the altar? Seest thou how faith wrought with his works, and by works was faith made perfect? . . . ye see then how that by works a man is justified, and not by faith only.'

"The testimony of the word of God is against this ensnaring doctrine of faith without works. It is not faith that claims the favor of heaven without complying with the conditions upon which mercy is to be granted, it is presumption; for genuine faith has its foundation in the promises and provisions of the Scriptures."

DA 671: " . . . The honor of God, the honor of Christ, is involved in the perfection of the character of His people."

CH 581: " . . . It is impossible for those who indulge the appetite to attain to Christian perfection . . . "

DA 789: "Order and perfection are seen in all His (Christ's) work."

5T 214: "It is left with us to remedy the defects in our characters, to cleanse the soul temple of every defilement. Then the latter rain will fall upon us as the early rain fell upon the disciples on the day of Pentecost."

IHP 145 (MS 5 1886): "It is a very difficult thing for one to understand himself. We must examine closely to see if there is not something that must be laid aside."

6

KH 229 (ST June 16, 1890): "The faith we are required to have is not a do-nothing faith; saving faith is that which works by love and purifies the soul . . . Faith and works will keep us evenly balanced, and make us successful in the work of perfecting Christian character."

GC 489: "He (Satan) is constantly seeking to deceive the followers of Christ with the fatal sophistry that it is impossible for them to OVERCOME."

SC 50: "The poor sufferer was helpless; he had not used his limbs for thirty-eight years. Yet Jesus bade him 'rise, take up thy bed, and walk.' The sick man might have said, 'Lord, if Thou wilt make me whole, I will obey Thy word.' But no, he believed Christ's word, believed that he was made whole, and he made the effort at once; he willed to walk, and he did walk. **He ACTED on the word of Christ, and God gave the POWER.** He was made whole."

A Solemn Appeal 29: "If Satan seeks to divert the mind from this to low and sensual things, bring it back again, and place it on eternal things; and when the Lord **sees the determined EFFORT made to retain only pure THOUGHTS, He will attract the MIND, like the magnet, and PURIFY** the thoughts, and enable them to cleanse themselves from every secret sin."

AA 531: "None need fail of attaining, in his sphere, to perfection of Christian character. By the sacrifice of Christ, provision has been made for the believer to receive all things that pertain to life and godliness. God calls upon us to reach the standard of perfection, and places before us the example of Christ's character. In His humanity, perfected by a life of constant resistance of evil, the Saviour showed that through co-operation with divinity, human beings may in this life attain to perfection of character. This is God's assurance to us that we too may obtain complete victory."

Redemption 86: " . . . He left to themselves the work of correcting the evils of their natures. He instructed them how to unite their human efforts with His divine power, and triumph through His strength over the sins that beset them."

CT 221: "It has been truly said, 'Show me your company, and I will show you your character."

COL 330: "Never should we lower the standard of righteousness in order to accommodate inherited or cultivated tendencies to wrongdoing. We need to understand that imperfection of character is sin."

7

9T 185: " . . . He (Jesus) came to the world Himself, in our behalf to work out a perfect character."

IHP 256 (MS 15, 1908): "Jesus **gained the victory** through **submission and faith in God.**"

RH Oct. 9, 1894: "The first step in obedience is to **surrender the will to God.**"

ST Jan. 16, 1896: "In human nature, Christ **developed a perfect character.** He was beset with the fiercest temptations, tempted on all points like as men, yet He developed a perfectly upright character. No taint of sin was found upon Him."

CT 222: "Strength of character consists of two things—POWER OF THE WILL and POWER OF SELF CONTROL."

PP 207: "God has elected a character in harmony with His law, and any one who shall reach the standard of His requirement, will have an entrance into the kingdom of glory."

COL 38: "He who by faith receives the word is receiving the very life and character of God."

TM 18: "The Lord Jesus is making experiments on human hearts through the exhibition of His mercy and abundant grace. He is effecting transformations so amazing that Satan, with all his triumphant boasting, with all his confederacy of evil united against God and the laws of His government, stands viewing them as a fortress impregnable to his sophistries and delusions. They are to him an incomprehensible mystery. The angels of God, seraphim and cherubim, the powers commissioned to cooperate with human agencies, look on with astonishment and joy, that fallen men, once children of wrath, are through the training of Christ, developing characters after the divine similitude, to be sons and daughters of God, to act an important part in the occupations and pleasures of heaven."

AA 482: "The work of gaining salvation is one of co-partnership, a joint operation. There is to be cooperation between God and the repentant sinner. This is necessary for the formation of right principles in the character. Man is to make earnest efforts to overcome that which hinders him from attaining to perfection. But he is wholly dependent upon God for success. Human effort of itself is not sufficient. Without the aid of divine power, it avails nothing. God works and man works. Resistance of temptation must come from man, who must draw his power from God."

5T 214: "Not one of us will ever receive the seal of God while our characters have one spot or stain upon them."

8

MAN IS WAITING ON GOD —
GOD IS WAITING ON MAN

1 T 619: "I was shown that if God's people make no efforts on their part, but wait for the refreshing to come upon them and remove their wrongs and correct their errors; if they depend upon that to cleanse them from filthiness of the flesh and spirit, and fit them to engage in the loud cry of the third angel, they will be found wanting. The refreshing or power of God comes only on those who have prepared themselves for it by doing the work which God bids them, namely, cleansing themselves from all filthiness of the flesh and spirit, perfecting holiness in the fear of God."

PP 248: "In order to receive God's help, man must realize his weakness and deficiency; he must apply his own mind to the great change to be wrought in himself; he must be aroused to earnest and persevering prayer and effort. WRONG HABITS AND CUSTOMS MUST BE SHAKEN OFF: and it is only by determined endeavor to correct these errors, and conform to right principles, that the victory can be gained. Many never attain to the position that they might occupy, because they wait for God to do for them that which He has given them power to do for themselves. All who are fitted for usefulness must be trained by the severest mental and moral discipline; and God will ASSIST them BY UNITING DIVINE POWER WITH HUMAN EFFORT."

RH April 11, 1880: "The pleasing fable that all there is to do is to believe, has destroyed thousands and tens of thousands, because many have called that faith which is not faith, but simply a dogma. Man is an intelligent, accountable, being. He is not to be carried as a passive burden by the Lord, but is to work in harmony with Christ. Man is to take up his appointed work in striving for glory, honor, and immortality. God calls upon man for the use of every talent He has lent them, the exercise of every power He his given them: for man can never be saved in disobedience and indolence."

TM 507: "Only those who are living up to the light they have will receive greater light. Unless we are daily advancing in the exemplification of the active Christian virtues, we shall not recognize the manifestation of the Holy Spirit in the latter rain. It may be falling on hearts all around us, but we shall not discern or receive it."

TM 399: "We may be sure that when the Holy Spirit is poured out, those who did not receive and appreciate the early rain, will not see or understand the value of the latter rain."

9

RH Nov. 13, 1913: "We profess to be pilgrims and strangers on earth, journeying to a better country, even an heavenly. If we indeed are but sojourners here, traveling to a land where none but the holy can dwell, we shall make it our first business to become acquainted with that country; we shall make **diligent inquiry as to the preparation needed**, the **manners**, and **character** which we must have, in order to become citizens there. Jesus, the King of that land, is pure and holy."

TM 507: "They expect that the lack will be supplied by the latter rain . . . They are making a terrible mistake."

FOOLISH VIRGINS

RH Aug. 19, 1890: "There are persons who have received the precious light of the righteousness of Christ, but they do not **act** upon it; **they are foolish virgins.**"

DA 309: "The **greatest deception** of the human mind in Christ's day was, that a **mere assent to the truth constitutes righteousness.** In all human experience, a theoretical knowledge of the truth has been proved to be insufficient for the saving of the soul. It does not bring forth the fruits of righteousness. A jealous regard for what is termed theological truth, often accompanies a hatred of genuine truth as made manifest in life."

COL 411: "The class represented by the foolish virgins are not hypocrites. They have a regard for the truth, they have advocated the truth, they are attracted to those who believe the truth; but they have not yielded themselves to the Holy Spirit's working. They have not fallen upon the Rock, Christ Jesus, and permitted their old nature to be broken up. . . . They have been content with a superficial work. They have not studied His character.

COL 307: "The parable of the wedding garment opens before us a lesson of the highest consequence. By the marriage is presented the union of humanity with divinity; the wedding garment represents the character which all must possess who shall be accounted fit guests for the wedding."

DA 88: "Because the life of Jesus condemned evil, He was opposed, both at home and abroad."

GCB 1901, 23: Thirteen years after the Minneapolis meeting, at the General Conference of 1901, Sister White said: "I feel a special interest in the movements and decisions that shall be made at this Conference regarding the things that should have been done years ago, and especially ten years ago when we were assembled in Conference, and the Spirit and power of God came into our meeting, testifying that God was ready to work for this people if they would come into working order. **The brethren assented to the light God had given, but . . . the light that was given was not acted upon** . . . year after year the same acknowledgment was made, but the principles which exalt a people were not woven into the work. . . ."

OHC (MS 9, 1899): "A mere assent to the truth is not enough. Daily we must live the truth."

ST July 29, 1902: **"Every one who by faith obeys God's commandments will reach the condition of sinlessness in which Adam lived before his transgression. When we submit ourselves to Christ, we live His life. This is what it means to be clothed with the garment of His righteousness."**

A PURIFIED AND PURGED MINISTRY TO OFFER "AN OFFERING IN RIGHTEOUSNESS"

Mal. 3:1-3: "Behold, I will send my messenger, and he shall prepare the way before me: and the Lord, whom ye seek, shall suddenly come to his temple, even the messenger of the covenant, whom ye delight in: behold, he shall come, saith the Lord of hosts.

But **who may abide the day of his coming?** and who shall stand when he appeareth? for he is like a refiner's fire, and like fuller's soap.

And **he shall sit as a refiner and purifier** of silver: and **he shall purify the sons of Levi, and purge them as gold and** silver, **that they may offer unto the Lord an offering in righteousness."**

FILB 293 (RH June 22, 1911): "There are those who will be glad to lull you to sleep in your carnal security, but I have a different work. My message is to alarm you, to bid you reform your lives and cease your rebellion against the God of the universe. Take the word of God, and see if you are in harmony with it. Is your character such as will bear the search of the heavenly investigation?"

11

RH April 8, 1890: "Those who are finally victorious will have seasons of terrible perplexity and trial in their religious life; but they must not cast away their confidence, for this is a part of their discipline in the school of Christ and it is essential in order that all dross may be purged away."

RH Feb. 11, 1890: "In times of trial, we must cling to God and His promises. Some have said to me 'Do you not get discouraged at times when you are under trial?' And I have answered: 'Yes, if by discouragement you mean sad or cast down.' 'Didn't you talk to anyone of your feelings?' 'No, there is a time for silence, a time to keep the tongue as with a bridle, and I was determined to utter no word of doubt or darkness, to bring no shade of gloom upon those with whom I was associated. I have said to my self, I will bear the Refiner's fire; I shall not be consumed. When I speak, it shall be of light; it shall be of faith and hope in God; it shall be of righteousness, of goodness, of the love of Christ my Saviour; it shall be to direct the minds of others toward heaven and heavenly things, to Christ's work in Heaven for us, and our work upon earth for Him."

NOTE: The coming to the temple, here mentioned, refers to Christ's coming to the Holy of Holies in 1844 for the work of the investigative judgment.

Therefore the "Sons of Levi" does not refer to the priesthood of the Old Testament, but to the ministry of God's remnant church from 1844 to the close of human probation.

The refining, purifying, and purging, must take place before we are able to offer "an offering in righteousness."

MM 12: "The sick are to be healed through the combined efforts of the human and the divine. Sin brings physical and spiritual disease and weakness, Christ has made it possible for us to free ourselves of this curse. The Lord promises by the medium of truth to renovate the soul. The Holy Spirit will make all who are willing to be educated, able to communicate the truth with power. It will renew every organ of the body, that God's servants may work acceptably and successfully. Vitality increases under the influence of the Spirit's action. Let us by this power lift ourselves into a higher, holier atmosphere, that we may do well our appointed work."

OHC 265 (MS 26, 1886): "Let us take care that we do nothing which will weaken physical, mental, or spiritual healthfulness, for God will not accept a tainted, diseased, corrupted sacrifice."

GC 473-474: "They will not by the indulgence of appetite or passion enfeeble or defile the offering which they present to their Heavenly Father."

CDF 49-50 (Sp. G IV, 148, 1864): ". . . After man has done all in his power to ensure health, by the denying of appetite and gross passions that he may possess a healthy mind, and a sanctified imagination, that he may render to God an offering in righteousness, then he is saved alone by a miracle of God's mercy, as was the ark upon the stormy billows. Noah had done all that God required of him in making the ark secure; then God performed that which man could not do, and preserved the ark by His miraculous power."

2T 549: "He is a perfect and holy example given for us to imitate. We cannot equal the pattern; but we shall not be approved of God if we do not copy it and, according to the ability which God has given, resemble it."

THE SCIENCE OF CHRISTIANITY:

SELF-MASTERY, AND MIND THERAPY

MH 453-454: "There is a science of Christianity to be mastered, — a science as much deeper, broader, higher than any human science as the heavens are higher than the earth. **The mind is to be disciplined, educated, trained;** for we are to do service for God in ways that are not in harmony with inborn inclination. **Hereditary and cultivated tendencies to evil must be overcome. Often the education and training of a lifetime must be discarded, that one may become a learner in the school of Christ. Our hearts must be educated to become steadfast in God. We are to form habits of thought that will enable us to resist temptation."**

KH 229 (ST June 16, 1890): "The faith we are required to have is not a do-nothing faith; saving faith is that which works by love and purifies the soul . . . Faith and works will keep us evenly balanced, and make us successful in the work of perfecting Christian character.

Ed 170: "The more we search the Bible, the deeper is our conviction that it is the word of the living God, and human reason bows before the Majesty of divine revelation."

CT 66: "When men have gone as far in scientific research as their limited powers will permit, there is still an infinity beyond what they can comprehend."

13

COL 108-109 "A student may go through all the grades of the schools and colleges of today. He may devote all his powers to acquiring knowledge. But, unless he has a knowledge of God, unless he obeys the laws that govern his being, he will destroy himself. By wrong habits he loses his power of self-appreciation. He loses self-control. He cannot reason correctly about matters that concern him most closely. He is reckless and irrational of his treatment of mind and body. By wrong habits he makes of himself a wreck. Happiness, he cannot have; for his neglect to cultivate pure, healthful principles places him under the control of habits that ruin his peace. His years of taxing study are lost; for he has destroyed himself. He has misused his physical and mental powers, and the temple of the body is in ruins. He is ruined for this life and for the life to come. By acquiring earthly knowledge he thought to gain a treasure; but by laying his Bible aside, he sacrificed a treasure worth everything else."

OHC 172 (ST Mar. 1, 1910): "Today, as in the past, all heaven is watching to see the church develop in the true science of salvation . . . "

TM 240: "The Lord does not propose to perform for us either the willing or the doing. This is our proper work. As soon as we earnestly enter upon the work, God's grace is given to work in us to will and to do, but never as a substitute for our effort. Our souls are to be aroused to cooperate. The Holy Spirit works the human agent, to work out our own salvation. This is the practical lesson the Holy Spirit is striving to teach us."

AA 482-483: "God wishes us to have the mastery over ourselves . . . Of ourselves, we are not able to bring the purposes and desires and inclinations into harmony with the will of God; 'but if we are willing to be made willing,' the Saviour will accomplish this for us, 'casting down imaginations; and every high thing that exalteth itself against the knowledge of God, and bringing into captivity every thought to the obedience of Christ."

IHP 27 (L 135, 1898): "The Spirit of God does not propose to do our part either in the willing or the doing . . . As soon as we incline our will to harmonize with God's will, the grace of Christ stands ready to cooperate with the human agent; but it will not be the substitute to do our work independent of our resolving and decidedly acting."

PK 486-487: "While God was working in Daniel and his companions 'to will and to do of His good pleasure,' they were working out their own salvation. Herein is revealed the outworking of the divine

14

principle of cooperation, without which no true success can be attained. Human effort avails nothing without divine power; and without human endeavor, divine effort is with many of no avail. To make God's grace our own, we must act our part. His grace is given to work in us to will and to do, but never as a substitute for our efforts."

2T 265: "The mind must be educated and disciplined to love purity."

2T 188: "Some need to discipline the mind by exercise. They should force it to think . . . Efforts must be made by every individual to educate the mind."

PP 248: "In order to receive God's help, man must realize his weakness and deficiency; he must apply his own mind to the great change to be wrought in himself; he must be aroused to earnest and persevering prayer and effort. WRONG HABITS AND CUSTOMS MUST BE SHAKEN OFF: and it is only by determined endeavor to correct these errors, and conform to right principles, that the victory can be gained. Many never attain to the position that they might occupy, because they wait for God to do for them that which He has given them power to do for themselves. All who are fitted for usefulness must be trained by the severest mental and moral discipline; and God will ASSIST them BY UNITING DIVINE POWER WITH HUMAN EFFORT."

OHC 265 (MS 60, 1894): "It is our duty to train and discipline the body. We are not to pamper the appetite . . . The sacred temple of the body must be kept pure and uncontaminated, that God's Holy Spirit may dwell therein."

3T 378: "You must then answer your own prayer as far as possible, by resisting temptation, and leave that which you cannot do for yourselves for Jesus to do for you."

2T 189: "The reason it is so difficult for men and women to live religious lives is because they do not exercise the mind unto godliness. It is trained to run in the opposite direction. Unless the mind is constantly exercised in obtaining spiritual knowledge, and in seeking to understand the mystery of godliness, it is incapable of appreciating eternal things, because it has no experience in that direction. This is the reason why nearly all consider it up-hill business to serve the Lord."

MH 452: "The struggle for conquest over self, for holiness and heaven, is a life-long struggle. Without continual effort and constant activity, there can be no advancement in the divine life, no attainment of the victor's crown."

AA 531: "God calls upon us to reach the standard of perfection, and places before us the example of Christ's character. In His humanity, perfected by a life of constant resistance of evil, the Saviour showed that through cooperation with divinity human beings may in this life attain to perfection of character. This is God's assurance to us that we too may obtain complete victory."

4T 626: "Those who abide in Jesus will be happy, cheerful, and joyful in God. A subdued gentleness will mark the voice, reverence for spiritual and eternal things will be expressed in the actions, and music, joyful music will echo from the lips, for it is wafted from the throne of God. This is the mystery of godliness, not easily explained, nonetheless felt and enjoyed."

MYP 98 (YI June 26, 1902): "Words cannot describe the peace and joy possessed by him who takes God at His word. Trials do not disturb him, slights do not vex him. Self is crucified."

5BC 1129 (Signs, May 10, 1899): "But although Christ's divine glory was for a time veiled and eclipsed by His assuming humanity, yet He did not cease to be God when He became man. The human did not take the place of the divine, nor the divine of the human. This is the mystery of godliness. The two expressions human and divine were, in Christ closely and **inseparably one,** and yet they had a distinct **INDIVIDUALITY.**"

MH 470-471: "THE DISCIPLINE OF TRIAL." "To live such a life, to exert such an influence, costs at every step, effort, self-sacrifice, discipline. It is because they do not understand this that many are so easily discouraged in the Christian life. Many who sincerely consecrate their lives to God's service are surprised and disappointed to find themselves, as never before, confronted by obstacles and beset by trials and perplexities. They pray for Christ-likeness of character, for a fitness for the Lord's work, and they are placed in circumstances that seem to call forth all the evil of their nature. Faults are revealed, of which they did not even suspect the existence. Like Israel of old, they question, "If God is leading us why do all these things come upon us?' "

"It is because God is leading them that these things come upon them. Trials and obstacles are the Lord's chosen methods of discipline and His appointed conditions of success. . . . In His providence He brings these persons into different positions and varied circumstances that they may discover in their character the defects which have been concealed from their own knowldge. He gives them opportunity to correct these defects, and to fit themselves for His service."

OHC 313 (L 9 1873): "We do not always consider that the sanctification we so earnestly desire and for which we pray so earnestly is brought about through the truth and, by the providence of God, in a manner we least expect. When we look for joy, behold there is sorrow. When we expect peace, we frequently have distrust and doubt, because we find ourselves plunged into trials we cannot avoid. In these trials we are having the answers to our prayers. In order for us to be purified, the fire of affliction must kindle upon us, and our will must be brought into conformity to the will of God. . . . God sees it best to put us under a course of discipline which is essential for us before we are fit subjects for the blessing we crave. . . . Perfection of character can be attained only through labor, conflict, and self-denial. . . . He brings us into positions which are the most trying to reveal what is in our hearts. To further the development of Christian graces He will place us in circumstances which will demand increased exertion on our part to keep our faith in lively exercise."

Ed 151: "All who in this world render true service to God or man receive a preparatory training in the school of sorrow. The weightier the trust and the higher the service, the closer is the test and the more severe the discipline."

3T 93: "All who are followers of Christ should deal with one another exactly as we wish the Lord to deal with us in our errors and weaknesses, for we are all erring, and need His pity and forgiveness."

MH 452: "The strongest evidence of man's fall from a higher state is the fact that it costs so much to return. The way of return can be gained only by hard fighting, inch by inch, hour by hour."

4T 32-33: "Man must work with his human power, aided by the divine power of Christ, to resist and to conquer at any cost to himself. In short man must overcome as Christ overcame. . . . This

17

could not be the case if Christ alone did all the overcoming. Man must do his part; he must be victor on his own account."

OHC 318 (L 2, 1889): "Oh, it is in the future life we shall see the tangles and mysteries of life that have so annoyed and disappointed our fond hopes, explained. We shall see that the prayers and hopes for certain things which have been withheld have been among our greatest blessings."

GC 474: "Every sinful gratification tends to benumb the faculties and deaden the mental and spiritual perceptions, and the word or the Spirit of God can make but a feeble impression upon the heart."

RH April 8, 1890: "Those who are finally victorious will have seasons of terrible perplexity and trial in their religious life; but they must not cast away their confidence, for this is a part of their discipline in the school of Christ and it is essential in order that all dross may be purged away."

MH 130-131: "Men and women need to be awakened to the duty of self-mastery, . . . Christ came to this world that man might have perfect mastery. . . . By becoming one with Christ, man is made free. Subjection to the will of Christ means restoration to perfect manhood. Man may stand conqueror of himself."

1SM 47 (MS 1, 1883): "Many a man professes to accept the testimonies, while they have no influence upon his character. His faults become stronger by indulgence until, having been often reproved and not heeding the reproof, he loses the power of self-control, and becomes hardened in a course of wrongdoing. If he is overworked, if weakness comes upon him, he has not moral power to rise above the infirmities of character which he did not overcome; they become his strongest points, and he is overborne by them."

CT 222: "Strength of character consists of two things—POWER OF THE WILL and POWER OF SELF CONTROL."

PP 421: "Exercise self-control under the greatest provocation."

2SM 52 (MS 1, 1890): "But we seem to sit as though we were paralyzed. God of heaven, wake us up!"

8T 313: "Paul's sanctification was a result of a constant conflict with self. He said, 'I die daily.' His will and his desires every day conflicted with duty and the will of God. Instead of following inclination, he did God's will, however crucifying to his own nature."

18

MH 452: "The struggle for conquest over self, for holiness and heaven, is a life-long struggle. Without continual effort and constant activity, there can be no advancement in the divine life, no attainment of the victor's crown."

DA 301: "The highest evidence of nobility in a Christian is self-control."

4T 32-33: "Man must work with his human power aided by the divine power of Christ, to resist and conquer at any cost to himself. In short, man must overcome as Christ overcame. . . . This could not be the case if Christ alone did all the overcoming. **Man must be victor on his own account.**"

MH 173: "They have lost their manhood, and this they must win back. Many have to battle against strong hereditary tendencies to evil. Unnatural cravings, sensual impulses, were their inheritance from birth."

CH 22-23: "Men have polluted the soul-temple, and God calls upon them to awake, and to strive with all their might to win back their God-given manhood."

9T 22: "The life that Christ lived in this world, men and women can live, through His power and under His instruction. In their conflict with Satan, they may have all the help that He had. They may be more than conquerors through Him who loved them and gave Himself for them."

THE LOST KINGSHIP TO BE RESTORED

MH 132: "The world needs a practical demonstration of what the grace of God can do in **restoring to human beings** their lost kingship, giving them mastery of themselves."

Ed 204: "Let the youth be impressed with the thought that they are to be masters, and not slaves. Of the kingdom within them God has made them rulers, and they are to exercise their Heaven-appointed kingship. When such instruction is faithfully given, the results will extend far beyond the youth themselves."

DA 301: "The highest evidence of nobility in a Christian is self-control."

FE 57: "The brute has only to be accustomed to submit to its master; but the child must be taught to control himself. The will must be trained to obey the dictates of reason and conscience."

THE SCIENCE OF REDEMPTION IS
SCIENCE AT THE TOP LEVEL

MS 69, 1897: "The science of redemption is as high as heaven, and its value is infinite. This truth is so broad, so deep, so high, that beside it all the wisdom of earth's wisest men sinks into insignificance."

THE OBJECT OF EDUCATION

Ed 15-16: "To restore in man the image of his Maker, to bring him back to the perfection in which he was created, to promote the development of body, mind, and soul, that the divine purpose in his creation might be realized — this was to be the work of redemption. This is to be the object of education, the great object of life."

5T 322: "To many, education means a knowledge of books, . . . the object of education is to restore the image of God in the soul. . . ."

2SM 32-33: "And while we cannot claim perfection of the flesh, we may have Christian perfection of the soul. Through the sacrifice made in our behalf, sins may be perfectly forgiven. Our dependence is not in what man can do; it is in what God can do for man through Christ. When we surrender ourselves wholly to God, and fully believe, the blood of Christ cleanses from all sin. The conscience can be freed from condemnation. Through faith in His blood, all may be made perfect in Christ Jesus. Thank God we are not dealing with impossibilities. We may claim sanctification. We may enjoy the favor of God. We are not to be anxious about what Christ and God think of us, but about what God thinks of Christ, our Substitute. Ye are accepted in the Beloved. The Lord shows, to the repenting, believing one, that Christ accepts the surrender of the soul, to be molded and fashioned after His own likeness."

Phil. 3:20-21: "For our conversation is in heaven: from whence also we look for the Saviour, the Lord Jesus Christ. Who shall change our vile body, that it may be fashioned like unto His glorious body, . . ."

GC 644-645: "But all arise with the freshness and vigor of eternal youth. . . . But the last lingering traces of the curse of sin will be removed, and Christ's faithful ones will appear 'in the beauty of the Lord our God,' in mind and soul and body reflecting the perfect image of our Lord."

IHP 154 (RH Jan. 11, 1912): "The Lord gave an important lesson to His people in all ages when to Moses on the mount He gave instruction regarding the building of the tabernacle. In that work He required perfection in every detail . . . Into all to which the Christian sets his hand should be woven the thought of the life eternal. If the work performed is agricultural or mechanical in its nature, it may still be after the pattern of the heavenly . . ."

OHC 337 (L 145, 1897): "To know what constitutes purity of mind, soul, and body is the highest class of education."

LLM 724 (B-84, May 7, 1909): "What was that power? It was the power resulting from the human nature uniting with the Divine, the power to take the teachings of Christ and follow them to the letter. In His resistance of evil and labor for others, Christ was giving to man an example of the highest education that it is possible for anyone to reach."

II

VICTORY AND SELF-MASTERY THROUGH AN UNDERSTANDING OF THE SON OF GOD IN HIS HUMANITY — THE PATTERN MAN

QOD 647 (YI Oct. 13, 1898): "The **humanity** of the Son of God is everything to us. It is the golden chain that binds our souls to Christ, and through Christ to God. This is to be **our study.** Christ was a real man; He gave proof of His humanity in becoming a man. Yet He was God in the flesh. When we approach this subject, we would do well to heed the words spoken by Christ to Moses at the burning bush, 'put off thy shoes from off thy feet, for the place whereon thou standest is holy ground.' We should come to this study with the **humility** of **a learner,** with a contrite heart. And the study of the **incarnation** of Christ is a fruitful field, which will repay the searcher who digs deep for hidden truth."

MH 501: "There was no rest for Him between the throne in heaven and the cross. His love for man led Him to welcome every indignity and suffer every abuse."

DA 363: "As a man He supplicated the throne of God till His **humanity** was charged with a heavenly current that should connect humanity with divinity. Through continual communion He received life from God that He might impart life to the world. His experience is to be ours."

Notebook Leaflets, Brown Leaflet No. 12 (MS 51, 1901): 'When men and women have formed characters which God can endorse, when they are ready for the final test, ready to be introduced into God's family, what service will stand highest in the estimation of Him who gave Himself a willing offering to save a guilty race? What enterprise will be most dear to the heart of infinite love? What work will bring the greatest satisfaction and joy to the Father and Son? The salvation of perishing souls . . . "

COL 196: "The value of a soul, who can estimate? Would you know it's worth, go to Gethsemane, and there watch with Christ through those hours of anguish, when He sweat as it were great drops of blood. Look upon the Saviour up-lifted on the cross.

Hear that dispairing cry, 'My God, My God, why has Thou forsaken me?' Look upon the wounded head, the pierced side, the marred feet. Remember, Christ risked all. For our redemption, heaven itself was imperiled. At the foot of the cross, remembering that for one sinner Christ would have laid down His life, you may estimate the value of a soul?"

Ev. 329: ". . . One soul is of more value than worlds beside."

6T 21-22: "One soul is of more value to heaven than a whole world of property, houses, lands, money. For the conversion of one soul we should tax our resources to the utmost."

Ev. 699 (ST Feb. 17, 1914): "The disciples did not ask for a blessing for themselves. They were weighted with the burden of souls. The gospel was to be carried to the ends of the earth, and they claimed the endowment of power that Christ had promised. Then it was that the Holy Spirit was poured out and thousands were converted in a day."

PP 68: "But the plan of redemption had a yet broader and deeper purpose than the salvation of man . . . it was to vindicate the character of God before the universe."

5BC 1128 (L 8, 1895): "Be careful, exceedingly careful, how you dwell upon the human nature of Christ. Do not set Him before the people as a man with propensities of sin. He is the second Adam. The first Adam was created a pure, sinless being, without a taint of sin upon him. He was made in the image of God. . . . But Jesus Christ took upon Himself HUMAN nature, and was tempted in all points as human nature is tempted. He could have sinned: He could have fallen, but not for one moment was there in Him an evil propensity. He was assailed with temptations in the wilderness as Adam was assailed with temptations in Eden."

SC 12: "Every soul was precious in His eyes. While He ever bore Himself with divine dignity, He bowed with tenderest regard to every member of the family of God. . . . This is the character of God."

PP 658: "There is no insanity so dreadful, so hopeless, as that of following human wisdom unguided by the wisdom of God."

7T 200: "The sin that is most nearly hopeless and incurable is pride of opinion, self-conceit. This stands in the way of all growth."

MH 453-454: "There is a SCIENCE of Christianity to be mastered, — a science as much deeper, broader, higher than any human science as the heavens are higher than the earth. THE MIND is to

23

be DISCIPLINED, educated, trained; for we are to do service for God in ways that are not in harmony with inborn inclination. Hereditary and cultivated TENDENCIES to evil must be overcome. Often the education and training of a lifetime must be discarded, that one may become a LEARNER in the school of Christ. Our hearts must be educated to become steadfast in God. We are to form habits of THOUGHT that will enable us to resist TEMPTATION."

QOD 65 (MS 76, 1903): "When we want a deep problem to study, let us fix our minds on the most marvelous thing that ever took place in earth or heaven — the incarnation of the Son of God."

Spl TM 47: "We cannot overestimate the importance of the union of divinity with humanity."

CHRIST HAD TWO NATURES, ONE DIVINE AND THE OTHER HUMAN, BUT THESE NATURES WERE KEPT DISTINCT

GCB Dec. 30, 1899: "Christ had two natures, the nature of a man, and the nature of God. In Him, divinity and humanity were combined. . . . He exhibited a perfect humanity, combined with diety; and by preserving each nature distinct, He has given to the world a representation of the character of God, and the character of a perfect man."

5BC 918 (MS 106, 1897): "The humanity of Christ could not be separated from His divinity."

DA 25: "Forever to retain His human nature . . ."

RH Oct. 1, 1889: "But we cannot explain how divinity was clothed with humanity."

5BC 1082 (RH Feb. 18, 1890): "Men may have a power to resist evil — a power that neither earth, nor death, nor hell can master; a power that will place them where they may overcome as Christ overcame. Divinity and humanity may be combined in them."

CONCERNING HIS NATURE, THE ANGEL SAID: Luke 1:35: "And the angel answered and said unto her, the Holy Ghost shall come upon thee, and the power of the Highest shall overshadow thee: therefore that holy thing which shall be born of thee shall be called the Son of God."

ST, Jan. 16, 1896: "The humanity of Christ is called that holy thing. The inspired record says of Christ, 'He did no sin,' that is 'knew no sin,' and 'in Him was no sin.' He was 'holy, harmless, undefiled, separate from sinners.' He tabernacled among men."

5BC 1128 (RH, Oct. 29, 1895): "Christ had not exchanged His divinity for humanity; but He had clothed His divinity with humanity.

5BC 1129 (ST, May 10, 1899): "But although Christ's divine glory was for a time veiled and eclipsed by His assuming humanity, yet He did not cease to be God when He became man. The human did not take the place of the divine, nor the divine of the human. **This is the mystery of godliness.** The two expressions human and divine were, in Christ closely and inseparably one, and yet **they had a distinct individuality.**"

2T 189: "The reason it is so difficult for men and women to live religious lives is because they do not exercise the mind unto godliness. It is trained to run in the opposite direction. Unless the mind is constantly exercised in obtaining spiritual knowledge, and in seeking to understand the mystery of godliness, it is incapable of appreciating eternal things, because it has no experience in that direction. This is the reason why nearly all consider it up-hill business to serve the Lord."

QOD 658 (YI, June 2, 1898): "In His human nature He maintained the purity of His divine character."

1SM 411 (RH Feb. 18, 1890): "If divine power does not combine with human effort, I would not give a straw for all that the greatest man could do."

MH 180: "Christ came to make us partakers of the divine nature, and His word declares that humanity combined with divinity does not commit sin."

4T 626: "Those who abide in Jesus will be happy, cheerful and joyful in God. A subdued gentleness will mark the voice, reverence for spiritual and eternal things will be expressed in the actions, and music, joyful music will echo from the lips, for it is wafted from the throne of God. This is the mystery of godliness, not easily explained, nonetheless felt and enjoyed.

MYP 98 (YI June 26, 1902) "Words cannot describe the peace and joy possessed by him who takes God at His word. Trials do not disturb him, slights do not vex him. Self is crucified."

MB 97: "God does not design that our will should be destroyed; for it is only through its exercise that we can accomplish what He would have us do.

"Our will is to be yielded to Him, that we may receive it again, purified and refined, and so linked in sympathy with the Divine that He can pour through us the tides of His love and power."

MYP 55 (RH, Feb. 10, 1903): "Our finite will must be brought into submission to the will of the Divine; the human will must be blended with the Divine. This will bring the Holy Spirit to our aid."

GCB Dec. 30, 1899: "Christ had two natures, the nature of a man, and the nature of God. In Him, divinity and humanity were combined. . . . He exhibited a perfect humanity, combined with deity; and by **preserving each nature distinct,** He has given to the world a representation of the character of **God,** and the character of a perfect **man."**

LLM 491: ". . . let us ever remember that while we seek to follow our pattern, Jesus Christ, we are to maintain our individuality."

Ed. 17: "Every human being, created in the image of God, is endowed with a power akin to that of the Creator — individuality, power to think and to do. — It is the work of true education to develop this power, to train the youth to be thinkers, and not mere reflectors of other men's thoughts."

THROUGH AN UNDERSTANDING OF THE HUMANITY OF CHRIST, MAN IS TO LEARN THE SECRET OF A VICTORIOUS LIFE

CHRIST'S CONCEPTION AND BIRTH

Matt. 1:20: "But while he thought on these things, behold, the angel of the Lord appeared unto him in a dream, saying, Joseph, thou son of David, fear not to take unto thee Mary thy wife: for that which is conceived (margin, **begotten)** in her is of the Holy Ghost."

1SM 250 (RH April 5, 1906): "Before the world was made, it was arranged that the divinity of Christ should be enshrouded in humanity. "A body," said Christ, "hast thou prepared me." (Heb. 10:15)

7BC 924 (RH June 25, 1895): "He lived out the character of God through the human body which God prepared for Him."

III

CHRIST, A TRUE HUMAN BEING,
BOTH PHYSICALLY AND SPIRITUALLY

7BC 929 (MS 1, 1892): "Christ's overcoming and obedience is that of a **TRUE human being.**" . . . the **completeness** of His humanity."

QOD 653 (RH April 5, 1906): "Christ did not make believe take human nature; He did **verily take it.** He did in **reality possess** human **nature.**"

QOD 647 (YI Oct. 13, 1898): "Christ was a **real man.**"

7BC 925 (L 97, 1898): He "came into the world in like manner as the human family" . . . "He **took human nature,** participating in the life of humanity."

MM 181 (B 62, 1902): "Upon His sinless nature He took our **sinful nature.**"

RH July 17, 1900: "The love that Christ manifested can not be comprehended by mortal man. It is a mystery too deep for the human mind to fathom. Christ did in reality unite the **offending nature of man with His own sinless nature,** because by this act of condescension He would be enabled to pour out His blessings in behalf of the fallen race. Thus He has made it possible for us to partake of His nature. By making Himself an offering for sin, He opened a way whereby human beings might be made one with Him. He placed Himself in man's position, becoming capable of suffering. The whole of His earthly life was a preparation for the altar."

QOD 664 (MS 92, 1899): "He clothed His divinity with humanity, and voluntarily took upon Him human nature making it possible to offer Himself as a ransom."

QOD 674 (ST June 5, 1893): "The only begotten Son of God took upon Him the nature of man, and established His cross between earth and heaven."

QOD 657 (RH Dec. 15, 1896): " . . . He was ever pure and undefiled; yet He took upon Him our sinful nature. Clothing His divinity with humanity, He sought to regain for man that which, by disobedience, Adam had lost for himself and for the world."

5T 235: "Jesus took upon Himself **man's nature.**"

OHC 17 (GCB April 23, 1901): "He took upon His divine soul the **RESULTS** of the transgression of God's law."

DA 117: He took "the **EFFECTS** of sin."

DA 48: "He was subject to the great law of **heredity.**"

MH 372: "The effect of **prenatal influences** is by many parents looked upon as a matter of little moment; but heaven does not so regard it."

Note: He was subject to maternal influence from conception to birth and through babyhood and childhood.

Good Health, Jan. 1880: "The **work of molding,** refining, and polishing **is the mother's.** The character of the child is to be developed."

Good Health, Feb. 1880: "The **basis of a right character** in the future man is made firm by habits of strict temperance in the mother **prior to the birth of her child.**"

Good Health, March 1880: "The mother's daily influence upon her children is preparing them for eternal life or death."

MH 372, 373: "If before the birth of her child she is self-indulgent, if she is selfish, impatient, and exacting, these traits will be reflected in the disposition of the child."

DA 69: "Through the **Holy Spirit** she received **wisdom to cooperate** with the heavenly agencies in the development of this child who could claim only God as His Father."

NOTE: How did Mary His mother exert this right influence and molding?

Mary's response to the Angel Gabriel was (Luke 1:38), "Behold the handmaiden of the Lord; be it unto me according to thy word." Here is shown the **complete submission** to God's plan for her, though she did not understand it. Here is **complete faith in God.** Joseph, too (Matt. 1:20, 24), **submitted** himself to God's purpose for him and Mary. She must have hid in her heart the Word of God that she might not sin. Psa. 119:11.

DA 512: "If we will live in communion with God, we too may expect the divine Spirit to **mould our little ones** from their earliest moments."

QOD 657 (L 97, 1898): "He was **born without a taint of** sin, but came into the world in like manner as the human family."

QOD 651 (L 8, 1895): "Not for a moment was there in Him an evil propensity."

DA 512: "Even the babe in its mother's arms may **dwell** under the shadow of the Almighty through **the faith of a praying mother.**"

5BC 1117 (YI Aug. 22, 1901): "In the sanctuary of the home Jesus received His education, not merely from His parents, but from His heavenly Father."

NOTE: This education was in gaining a knowledge of the Word of God, the Old Testament Scriptures, through hearing His mother telling the stories, reciting the promises. Through prayer and practice He learned, and this molded His character.

29

Psa. 119:11: "Thy word have I hid in my heart that I might not sin against thee."

NOTE: The Holy Spirit guided Mary in her influence upon her child, and she cooperated. See Luke 2:52. "He grew in favor with God and man." Thus through the faithful submission and daily cooperation of His parents the child lived under the shadow of the Almighty and was filled with the influence of the Holy Spirit. He was surrounded with an "atmosphere of grace."

The home life of Jesus, which laid the basis for His human character, is a model for every home. Thus Jesus became a pattern and example for all ages of human life.

Luke 2:51: "And he went down with them and came to Nazareth, and was subject to them."

DA 123: "He was fitted for the conflict by the indwelling of the Holy Spirit."

RH Dec. 24, 1885: "Jesus clothed His divinity with humanity that He might have an experience in all that pertains to human life. . . . **He became a child and in His life we find an example of what is the proper development of childhood.**"

NOTE: At some point of age in early childhood (2-3 years) He began to make His own decisions. As Isa. 8:15 says, "To refuse the evil and to choose the good." At this time, by His "own desire and consent," (COL 411), He yielded Himself to God to serve Him only and to resist Satan. With this personal decision He was filled with the Spirit, and was wholly turned to God. This was a spiritual birth of the Holy Spirit. This is to be our experience in a true conversion.

Through constant — instant — submission to the Spirit and cooperation with the Spirit's guidance, He lived a life of obedience and service. This infilling came through His own "desire and consent," through asking for it (Matt. 7:7). By daily maintaining this cooperation He could resist every temptation of Satan to sin by failing to exercise faith in God's Word, and then to doubt it and depart from it. Joshua 1:8; Ps. 119:15, 48, 148.

DA 68: "The powers of mind and body developed gradually, in keeping with the laws of childhood."

RH Oct. 9, 1900: "The lessons given during the first years of life determine the future of the child. This great work is a work that can be done only by the Holy Spirit. And the Holy Spirit cannot do this unless parents welcome Christ into their hearts as an abiding guest. The Holy Spirit must be honored in the temple of the soul where He delights to dwell."

CG 22 (ST April 16, 1896): "An angel from heaven came to instruct Zacharias and Elizabeth as to how they should train and educate their child, so as to work in harmony with God in preparing a messenger to announce the coming of Christ. As parents they were to faithfully co-operate with God in forming such a character in John as would fit him to perform the part God had assigned him as a competent worker.

"John was the son of their old age, he was a child of miracle, and the parents might have reasoned that he had a special work to do for the Lord and the Lord would take care of him. But the parents did not thus reason; they moved to a retired place in the country, where their son would not be exposed to the temptations of city life, or induced to depart from the counsel and instruction which they as parents would give him. They acted their part in developing a character in the child that would in every way meet the purpose for which God had designed his life. . . . They sacredly fulfilled their obligation."

Regard Children as a Trust. — "Parents are to look upon their children as entrusted to them of God to be educated for the family above. Train them in the fear and love of

31

God; for " 'the fear of the Lord is the beginning of wisdom.' "

CG 22 (MS 103, 1902): — **Parents to Qualify as Christian Teachers.** — "The work of parents, which means so much, is greatly neglected. Awake, parents, from your spiritual slumber and understand **that the very first teaching the child receives is to be given to him by you.** You are to teach your little one to know Christ. This work you must do before Satan sows his seeds in their hearts. Christ calls the children, and they are to be led to Him, educated in habits of industry, neatness, and order."

IV

HOW CHRIST MAINTAINED A SINLESS CHARACTER
IN A FALLEN, SINFUL, HUMAN NATURE

The purpose of Christ in taking humanity was to set a pattern for the converted or born-again man, showing him how to obtain victory over the flesh, the devil, and the world.

YI Oct. 20, 1886: ". . . (He) became like one of us except in sin, that **His life** and character should be a **pattern for all** to copy . . ."

MH 181: "The Saviour overcame to show man how he may overcome."

RH Feb. 18, 1890: "Christ came to reveal the source of His power, that man might never rely on his unaided capabilities. Those who would overcome must put to the tax every power of their being. They must agonize on their knees before God for divine power."

AA 531: "God calls upon us to reach the standard of perfection, and places before us the example of Christ's character. In His humanity, perfected by a life of constant resistance of evil, the Saviour showed that through cooperation with divinity human beings may in this life attain to perfection of character. This is God's assurance to us that we too may obtain complete victory."

YI June 2, 1898: "In His human nature He maintained the purity of His divine character."

DA 24: "As one of us, He was to give an example of obedience. For this He took upon Himself our nature, and passed through our experiences. In all things it behooved Him to be made like unto His brethren. If we had to bear anything which Jesus did not endure, then upon this point Satan would represent the power of God as insufficient for us. Therefore Jesus was 'in all points tempted like as we are.' He endured every trial to which we are subject. And He exercised in His own behalf no power that is not freely offered to us. As man He met temptation and overcame in the strength given Him from God."

Redemption, or the Ascension of Christ, 78: "He had wrought out a righteous character on earth as an example for man to follow."

FE 442 (Sp Ed 1896): "From the earliest times the faithful in Israel had given much attention to the matter of education. The Lord had directed that the children, even from babyhood, should be taught of His goodness and His greatness, especially as revealed in His law, and shown in the history of Israel. Through song and prayer, and the lessons from the Scriptures adapted to the opening mind, fathers and mothers were to instruct their children that the law of God is an expression of His character, and that as they received the principles of the law into the heart, the image of God was traced on mind and soul. In both the school and the home, much of the teaching was oral, but the youth also learned to read the Hebrew writings; and the parchment rolls of the Old Testament Scriptures were open to their study."

HIS EDUCATION

5BC 1117 (YI Sept. 8, 1898): "He was an example of what all children may strive to be if parents will seek the Lord most earnestly, and if children will cooperate with their parents."

5BC 1117, 1118 (YI Aug. 22, 1901): "In the sanctuary of the home Jesus received His education, not merely from His parents, but from His heavenly Father. As He grew older God opened to Him more and more of the great work before Him."

Ed 44: "A knowledge of God, fellowship with Him in study and in labor, likeness to Him in character, were to be the source, the means, and the aim of Israel's education. . . . the education imparted by God to the parents, and by them to be given to their children."

CG 66 (L 9, 1904): "From the rules that God has given for the guidance of parents and children there can be no sinful swerving. God expects parents to give their children a training that is in accordance with the principles of His word."

5BC 1116 (YI Sept. 8, 1898): "Jesus was instructed in accordance with the divine character of His mission."

CG 66 (L 356, 1897): "The work of education in the home, if it is to accomplish all that God designs it shall, demands that parents be diligent students of the Scriptures."

Prov. 3:7: "Fear the Lord, and depart from evil."

Prov. 5:7: "Depart not from the words of my mouth."

Prov. 16:6: ". . . by the fear of the Lord men depart from evil."

Prov. 22:6: "Train up a child in the way he should go, and when he is old, he will not depart from it."

CG 66 (L 356, 1897): "They have been educated to regard the word of God as supreme, and they will test every experience that comes to them by the law and the testimony."

SC 88: "Fill the whole heart with the words of God."

NOTE: Joseph and Mary had made full surrender of their wills and lives to God in accepting the mission of the parentage of Jesus. This same spirit of submission was imparted to the child Jesus in the kind of education they gave Him under the guidance and help of the Holy Spirit and the heavenly agencies. This education was in a knowledge of the word of God which is the beginning of wisdom.

This led Him to a full surrender of Himself to God when the moment in childhood came to make such a decision for Himself. The complete devotion of the parents to God's will made its impress upon His mind and prepared Him for His decision to serve His heavenly Father.

Jesus' education was a perfect example of God's plan for the education of all children.

How did Jesus obtain the inclination to obedience to God and to His word?

The place of the parents in the formation of a disposition to serve God only, should be noted.

What was the education given Him?

4T 439: "It will be well to remember that tendencies of character are transmitted from parents to children."

PP 561: "The child will be affected for good or for evil by the habits of the mother. . . . The effect of pre-natal influences has been by many lightly regarded."

CD 219: ". . . she transmits to them her own qualities, her own strong or weak traits of character."

MH 372: "She . . . imparts to it also mental and spiritual influences that tend to the shaping of mind and character."

CG 169 (ST Sept. 10, 1894): "Here is your work, parents, to develop the characters of your children in harmony with the precepts of the word of God. This work should come first, for eternal interests are here involved."

NOTE: We believe Joseph and Mary obeyed this instruction fully in their care of the baby Jesus. This was done by submission to the Spirit's guidance and in full cooperation with the Spirit and the angels.

CG 169 (ST Nov. 24, 1881): "God has given parents their work, to form the characters of their children after the divine pattern. By His grace they can accomplish the task."

ST Aug. 15, 1906: "Infant children are a mirror for the mother in which she may see reflected her own habits and deportment."

NOTE: Whatever traits of character she wishes to see developed in them, she must cultivate in herself.

CG 487: "The first lesson that children are to be taught is that God is their Father. This lesson should be given them in their earliest years."

CG 486: "As soon as a child can love and trust his mother, then can he love and trust Jesus as the Friend of his mother."

MH 460: "From the earliest dawn of reason they should be made familiar with the name and life of Jesus. Their first lesson should teach them that God is their Father. Their first training should be that of loving obedience."

ST Mar. 11, 1891: "The little ones, before they are a year old, hear and understand what is spoken in reference to themselves, and know to what extent they are to be indulged."

FE 439, 440: "He began at a very early age to act for Himself in the formation of His character. While His mother was His first human teacher, He was constantly receiving an education from His Father in heaven. Jesus, under the Divine Teacher, studied the word of God, pure and uncorrupted. He studied also the great lesson book of nature."

NOTE: From conception Jesus was influenced by the atmosphere of the prayer life of His parents. Their minds were filled with God's words. They searched the Scriptures under the influence of the Spirit to understand the nature and work of their child.

7BC 929 (M 1, 1892): "Jesus, the world's Redeemer, could only keep the commandments of God in the same way that humanity can keep them."

Psalms 119:11: "Thy word have I hid in mine heart, that I might not sin against thee."

Psalms 17:4: "By the word of thy lips I have kept me from the paths of the destroyer."

SC 88: "Fill the whole heart with the Words of God."

Ed 258: "To live thus by the word of God, means the surrender to Him of the whole life."

Deut. 8:3: "That He might make thee know that man doth not live by bread only, but by every word that proceedeth out of the mouth of the Lord doth man live."

GC 51: "At every assault, Christ presented the shield of eternal truth, saying, 'It is written.' To every suggestion of the adversary, He opposed the wisdom and power of the word."

NOTE: The words of Moses in Deuteronomy and of David in the Psalms must have been impressed upon His baby mind from the very beginning.

CG 26 (GH July, 1880): "Education begins with the infant in its mother's arms."

NOTE: He received an education such as is described for us today in the writings of Mrs. E. G. White — Child Guidance and Adventist Home.

9T 68: "To every temptation He presented the word of the Lord. 'It is written' was His never failing weapon. We, as the representatives of Christ, are to meet every thrust of the enemy with the word of the living God."

9T 279: "Christ clothed His divinity with humanity, and lived a life of prayer and self-denial and of daily battle with temptation, that He might help those who today are assailed by temptation."

Ed 80: "But the life of Jesus was a life of constant trust, sustained by continual communion."

FE 440: "Communion with God, a complete surrender of the soul to Him, in fulfilling His word irrespective of false education or the customs or traditions of His time, marked the life of Jesus."

7T 251: "Christ Himself was much in prayer. Whenever He had opportunity, He went apart to be alone with God."

DA 362: "Yet how often He was found in prayer. How constant was His communion with God."

DA 363: "He was wholly dependent upon God, and in the secret place of prayer He sought divine strength, that He might go forth braced for duty and trial."

DA 363: "As a man He supplicated the throne of God till His humanity was charged with a heavenly current that should connect humanity with divinity. Through continual communion He received life from God that He might impart life to the world. His experience is to be ours."

DA 664 "His perfect humanity is that which all His followers may possess if they will be in subjection to God as He was."

SD 136 (YI April, 1873): "The strength of Christ was in prayer."

Ed 259 "It was in hours of solitary prayer that Jesus in His earth-life received wisdom and power."

5T 161: "Remember that He was often in prayer, and His life was constantly sustained by fresh inspirations of the Holy Spirit."

5BC 1117 (ST July 30, 1896): "Firm and steadfast was His purpose to do right."

Psalms 5:1-3: 'Give ear to my words, O Lord, consider my meditation. Hearken unto the voice of my cry, O king, and my God, for unto Thee will I pray. My voice shalt thou hear in the morning, O Lord; in the morning will I direct my prayer unto thee, and will look up."

Psalms 59: 16, 17: "But I will sing of thy power; Yea, I will sing aloud of thy mercy in the morning; for thou hast been my defense and refuge in the day of my trouble. Unto Thee, O my strength, will I sing, for God is my defense and the God of my mercy."

Isaiah 50:4: "The Lord God hath given me the tongue of the learned, that I should know how to speak a word to him that is weary; He wakeneth morning by morning, He wakeneth mine ear to hear as the learned."

DA 73: "Often He expressed the gladness of His heart by singing Psalms and heavenly songs. Often the dwellers in Nazareth heard His voice raised in praise and thanksgiving to God. He held communion with heaven in song."

5BC 1117 (YI Sept. 8, 1898): "He welcomed the morning light. He listened to the lark caroling forth music to its God, and joined His voice with the voice of praise and thanksgiving."

DA 70: "Every child may gain knowledge as Jesus did."

NOTE: He gained knowledge from a mother who lived in submission to the Spirit and in cooperation with the angels.

9T 22: "The life that Christ lived in this world, men and women can live through His power and under His instruction. In their conflict with Satan, they may have all the help that He had. They may be more than conquerors through Him who loved them and gave Himself for them."

OHC 99 (L 186, 1902): ". . . He (Christ) must be exemplified in the minutest details of everyday service . . ."

OHC 99 (L 186, 1902): "As Christ the Pattern is constantly kept before the mind's eye, new habits will be formed, powerful hereditary and cultivated tendencies will be subdued and overcome, self-esteem will be laid in the dust, old habits of thought will be constantly resisted, love for the supremacy will be seen in its real, despicable character, and will be overcome."

2T 549: "He is a perfect and holy example given for us to imitate. We cannot equal the pattern; but we shall not be approved of God if we do not copy it and, according to the ability which God has given, resemble it."

5BC 1081 (RH June 10, 1890): "Christ has redeemed Adam's disgraceful fall, and has perfected a character of perfect obedience, and left an example for the human family, that they may imitate the pattern."

GC 510: "Satan assailed Christ with his fiercest and most subtle temptations; but he was repulsed in every conflict. Those battles were fought in our behalf; those victories make it possible for us to conquer. Christ will give strength to all who seek it. . . . The fact that Christ has conquered should inspire His followers with courage to fight manfully the battle against sin and Satan."

RH May 16, 1907: "The same devotion, the same self-sacrifice, the same subjection to the claims of the word of God, that are manifest in the life of Christ, must be seen in the lives of His servants."

NOTE: How could it occur that Jesus was born without a taint of sin, but came into the world in like manner as the human family?
His parents lived such a life of close communion with God that they were kept from sin, and so imparted no evil influence or inclination to sin during pre-natal development and during babyhood and childhood education and training. In this they and their child became a perfect pattern for us.

ST Nov. 9, 1904: "Christ came to our world to live a life of stainless purity, to show sinners that in His strength they too can obey God's holy precepts, the laws of His kingdom."

CT 178: "The example of Jesus is a light to the young, as well as to those of more mature years; for His was a representative childhood and youth. From His earliest years His example was perfect.

As a little child He was obedient to His parents, and to the laws of nature; 'and the grace of God was upon Him.' He studied the word of God until He became familiar with its sayings."

CT 178: "Even in His childhood, His life and all His habits were in harmony with the Scriptures, and He was skillful in their use."

5BC 1117 (YI Aug. 22, 1901): "He has left a perfect example for childhood, youth, and manhood."

MH 180: "The Saviour took upon Himself the infirmities of humanity, and lived a sinless life, that men might have no fear that because of the weakness of human nature they could not overcome. Christ came to make us 'partakers of the divine nature, and His life declares that humanity, combined with divinity, does not commit sin."

7BC 929 (MS 141, 1901): "Those who claim that it was not possible for Christ to sin, cannot believe that He really took upon Himself human nature. But was not Christ actually tempted, not only by Satan in the wilderness, but all through His life, from childhood to manhood? In all points He was tempted as we are, and because He successfully resisted temptation under every form, He gave man the perfect example, and through the ample provision Christ has made, we may become partakers of the divine nature, having escaped the corruption which is in the world through lust.

"Jesus says, 'To him that overcometh will I grant to sit with me in my throne,.even as I also overcame, and am set down with my Father in His throne.' Here is the beginning of our confidence which we must hold steadfast unto the end. If Jesus resisted Satan's temptations, He will help us to resist. He came to bring divine power to combine with human effort.

"Jesus was free from all sin and error; there was not a trace of imperfection in His life or character. He maintained spotless purity under circumstances the most trying. True, He declared, 'There is none good but one, that is, God'; but again He said, 'I and my Father are one.' Jesus speaks of Himself as well as the Father as God, and claims for Himself perfect righteousness."

7BC 929 (MS 1, 1897): "Christ's overcoming and obedience is that of a true human being. In our conclusions, we make many mistakes because of our erroneous views of the human nature of our Lord. When we give to His human nature a power that it is not possible for man to have in his conflicts with Satan, we destroy the completeness of His humanity. His imputed grace and power He gives to all who receive Him by faith."

40

"The obedience of Christ to His Father was the same obedience that is required of man. Man cannot overcome Satan's temptations without divine power to combine with his instrumentality. So with Jesus Christ; He could lay hold of divine power. He came not to our world to give the obedience of a lesser God to a greater, but as a man to obey God's holy law, and in this way He is our example. The Lord Jesus came to our world, not to reveal what a God could do, but what a man could do, through faith in God's power to help in every emergency. Man is, through faith, to be a partaker in the divine nature, and to overcome every temptation wherewith he is beset.

"The Lord now demands that every son and daughter of Adam, through faith in Jesus Christ, serve Him in human nature which we now have. The Lord Jesus has bridged the gulf that sin has made. He has connected earth with heaven, and finite man with the infinite God. Jesus, the world's Redeemer, could only keep the commandments of God in the same way that humanity can keep them."

V

CHRIST DEVELOPED THE SINLESS CHARACTER
WHICH ADAM SHOULD HAVE DEVELOPED

QOD 650 (ST June 29, 1898): "Christ came to the earth, taking humanity and standing as man's representative, to show in the controversy with Satan, that man as God created him, **connected with the Father and the Son,** could obey every divine requirement."

QOD 650 (YI June 2, 1889): "Christ is called the second Adam. He began where the first Adam began. Willingly He passed over the ground where Adam fell, and redeemed Adam's failure."

MH 180: "Christ came to make us partakers of the divine nature, and His word declares that **humanity combined with divinity does not commit sin.**"

COL 320: "But Christ came in the form of humanity and by His perfect obedience He proved that humanity and divinity combined can obey every one of God's precepts."

Special Testimonies on Ed. 33: "We are God's workmanship, and His word declares that we are 'fearfully and wonderfully made.' **He has prepared this living habitation for the mind; it is** 'curiously wrought,' **a TEMPLE** which the Lord Himself has fitted up for the indwelling of the Holy Spirit."

7BC 926 (Letter 121, 1897): "**That He might restore in man the original mind which he lost in Eden.**"

THE SANCTUARY REVEALS THE PURPOSE
FOR THE HUMAN SOUL

Ed 36: "Through Christ was to be fulfilled the purpose of which the tabernacle was a symbol, — . . . In all, God desired His people to read **His purpose for the human soul.**"

DA 161: "From eternal ages it was God's purpose that every **created** being, from the bright and holy seraph to man, should be a temple for the indwelling of the Creator."

QOD 651 (YI April 25, 1901): "He vanquished Satan in the same nature over which in Eden Satan obtained the victory . . . He overcame in human nature relying upon God for power."

RH July 28, 1874: "Christ in the wilderness of temptation, stood in Adam's place to bear the test he failed to endure."

QOD 653 (ST Dec. 9, 1897): "His spiritual nature was free from every taint of sin."

QOD 651 (ST June 9, 1898): "We should have no misgivings in regard to the perfect sinlessness of the human nature of Christ."

ST Jan. 16, 1896: "The humanity of Christ is called that holy thing. The inspired record says of Christ, 'He did no sin,' that is 'knew no sin,' and 'in Him was no sin.' He was 'holy, harmless, undefiled, separate from sinners.' He tabernacled among men."

7BC 925 (MS 21, 1892): "He came as a helpless babe, bearing the humanity we bear. 'As the children are partakers of flesh and blood, He also Himself likewise took part of the same; He could not come in the form of an angel: for unless He met man as man and testified by His connection with God that divine power was not given to Him in a different way to what it will be given to us, He could not be a perfect example for us.' "

CHRIST TOOK SINFUL NATURE THROUGH
MARY HIS MOTHER

MM 181: "He took upon His sinless nature our sinful nature, that He might know how to succor them that are tempted."

5BC 1131 (ST June 9, 1898): "In taking upon Himself human nature in its fallen condition, Christ did not in the least participate in its sin."

QOD 653 (RH April 5, 1906): "He was the Son of Mary; He was the seed of David according to human descent."

QOD 653 (RH July 28, 1874): "Christ bore the sins and infirmities of the race as they existed when He came to the earth to help man. In behalf of the race, with the weaknesses of fallen man upon Him, He was to stand the temptations of Satan upon all points wherewith man would be assailed."

QOD 653 (RH April 5, 1906): "Christ did not 'make believe' take human nature; He did verily take it. He did in reality possess human nature. 'As the children are partakers of flesh and blood, He also Himself likewise took part of the same.' He was the Son of Mary; He was of the seed of David according to human descent."

DA 48: "It would have been an almost infinite humiliation for the Son of God to take man's nature even when Adam stood in his innocency in Eden. But Jesus accepted humanity when the race had been weakened by four thousand years of sin. Like every child of Adam **He accepted the results of the working of the great law of heredity.** What these results were, is shown in the history of His earthly ancestors. He came with such a heredity to share our sorrows, and give us the **example of a sinless life.**"

ST Sept. 24, 1902: "He did not know sin by the experience of sinning; but he bore the terrible weight of the guilt of the whole world."

DA 117: "In our humanity, Christ was to redeem Adam's failure. But when Adam was assailed by the tempter, none of the effects of sin were upon him. . . . It was not thus with Jesus when He entered the wilderness to cope with Satan. For four thousand years the race had been decreasing in physical strength, in mental power, and in moral worth; and **Christ took upon Him the infirmities of degenerate humanity. Only thus could He rescue man** from the lowest depths of his degradation. Many claim that it was impossible for Christ to be overcome by temptation. Then He could not have been placed in Adam's position; He could not have gained the victory that Adam failed to gain. If we have in any sense a more trying conflict than had Christ, then He would not be able to succor us. But our

Saviour took humanity, with all its liabilities. He took the nature of man, with the possibility of yielding to temptation. We have nothing to bear which He has not endured."

TM 173: "What Christ was in His perfect humanity, we must be; for we must form characters for eternity."

RH July 28, 1874: "Christ in the wilderness of temptation, stood in Adam's place to bear the test he failed to endure."

2T 355: "We believe without a doubt that Christ is soon coming. . . . When He comes He is not to cleanse us of our sins, to remove from us the defects in our characters, or to cure us of the infirmities of our tempers and dispositions. If wrought for us at all, this work will all be accomplished before that time. When the Lord comes, those who are holy will be holy still. Those who have preserved their bodies and spirits in holiness, in sanctification and honor, will then receive the finishing touch of immortality."

RH July 28, 1874: "Christ bore the sins and infirmities of the race as they existed when He came to the earth to help man. In behalf of the race, with the weaknesses of fallen man upon Him, He was to stand the temptation of Satan upon all points wherewith man would be assailed.

ST June 17, 1897: "Had He not been fully human, Christ could not have been our substitute. He could not have worked out in humanity that perfection of character which it is the privilege of all to reach. . . . In His humanity, He laid hold of the divinity of God: and this every member of the human family has the privilege of doing. Christ did nothing that human nature may not do if it partakes of the divine nature."

1SM 47 (MS 1, 1883): "Many a man professes to accept the testimonies, while they have no influence upon his life or character. His faults become stronger by indulgence until, having been often reproved and not heeding the reproof, he loses the power of self-control, and becomes hardened in a course of wrongdoing. If he is overworked, if weakness comes upon him, he has not moral power to rise above the infirmities of character which he did not overcome; they become his strongest points, and he is overborne by them."

5BC 1113 (MS 131, 1897): "Humanity died; divinity did not die . . . Only He who alone hath immortality. . . . "

Webster's (International) immortal: 1. Not mortal; exempt from liability to die; undying; imperishable; everlasting . . . exempt from death.

DA 49: "He permitted Him to meet life's peril in common with every human soul, to fight the battle as every child of humanity must fight it, at the risk of failure and eternal loss"

RH Jan. 24, 1893: "Some will not make a right use of the doctrine of justification by faith. They will present it in a **ONE-SIDED** manner, making everything of faith and belittling works. Others will seize the points that have a leaning toward error, and will ignore works altogether. Now genuine faith always works by love; it supplies a motive power. Faith is **not an opiate, but a stimulant.** . . . Looking to Calvary will not quiet your soul into non-performance of duty, but will create faith that will work, purifying the soul from all selfishness. In laying hold of Christ by faith, we but just begin our work. Every man has corrupt and sinful habits, that must be overcome through vigorous warfare. Every soul must fight the fight of faith."

4T 32-33: "Man must work with his human power aided by the divine power of Christ, to resist and conquer at any cost to himself. In short, man must overcome as Christ overcame. . . . This could not be the case if Christ alone did all the overcoming. Man must be victor on his own account."

MH 452: "The strongest evidence of man's fall from a higher state is the fact that it costs so much to return. The way of return can be gained only by hard fighting, inch by inch, hour by hour."

Heb. 10:5: "Wherefore when he cometh into the world, he saith, sacrifice and offering thou wouldest not, but a body hast thou prepared me."

Phil. 2:7: He "was made in the likeness of men."

Heb. 2:14-17: "Forasmuch then as the children are partakers of flesh and blood, **He also Himself likewise took part of the same;** that through death He might destroy him that had the power of death, that is, the devil; and delivere them who through fear of death were all their lifetime subject to bondage. For verily He took not on Him the nature of angels; but **He took on Him the seed of Abraham.** Wherefore in all things it behooved Him to be **made like unto His brethren,** that He might be a merciful and faithful high priest in things pertaining to God, to make reconciliation for the sins of the people."

RH Dec. 15, 1896: "Clad in the vestments of humanity, the Son of God came down to the level of those He wished to save. In Him was no guile or sinfulness; He was ever pure and undefiled; yet **He took upon Him our sinful nature.** Clothing His divinity with humanity, that He might associate with fallen humanity, He sought to regain for man that which, by disobedience, Adam lost for himself and for the world."

RH July 28, 1874: "Christ bore the sins and infirmities of the race as they existed when He came to earth to help man. In behalf of the race, with the weaknesses of fallen man upon Him, He was to stand the temptations of Satan upon all points wherewith man would be assailed."

5BC 1131 (ST June 9, 1898) "In taking upon Himself **human** nature **in its fallen condition,** Christ did not in the least participate in its sin."

QOD 666 (Letter 97 — 1898): "He was born without a taint of sin, but came into the world in like manner as the human family."

MM 181: "He took upon His sinless nature our sinful nature, that He might know how to succor those that are tempted."

DA 172: "The Christian's life is not a modification or improvement of the old, but a transformation of nature. There is a death to self and sin, and a new life altogether. This change can be brought about only by the effectual working of the Holy Spirit."

Redemption, or the Teaching of Christ, Calvary 82: ". . . Christ was the prince of sufferers; but it was not bodily anguish that filled Him with horror or dispair; it was a sense of the malignity of sin, a knowledge that man had become so familiar with sin that he did not realize its enormity, that it was so deeply rooted in the human heart as to be difficult to eradicate."

DA 323-324: "When the soul surrenders itself to Christ, a new power takes possession of the **new heart.** A change is wrought which man can never accomplish for himself. It is a supernatural work, bringing a supernatural element into human nature."

2 Cor. 5:17: "Therefore if any man be in Christ, he is **a new creature.**"

RH June 29, 1897: "The Holy Spirit is the source of all power, and works as a living, active, agent in the new life created in the soul. The Holy Spirit is to be in us a divine indweller."

RH April 1, 1875: "Christ was put to the closest test requiring the strength of all His faculties to resist the inclination when in danger, to use His power to deliver Himself from peril and triumph over the power of the prince of darkness. It was as difficult for Him to keep the level of humanity as it was for men to rise above the level of their depraved natures and be partakers of the divine nature."

MH 452: "The struggle for conquest over self, for holiness and heaven, is a life-long struggle. Without continual effort and constant activity, there can be no advancement in the divine life, no attainment of the victor's crown."

OHC 91 (L 135, 1898): "And it is the very hardest, sternest conflict which comes with the purpose and hour of great resolve and decision of the human to incline the will and way to Gods will and God's way. Man is allotted a part in this great struggle for everlasting life; . . . It will require a struggle to break through the powers of darkness, but the Spirit that works in him can and will accomplish this. But man is no passive instrument to be saved in indolence. He is called upon to strain every muscle in the struggle for immortality; yet it is God that supplies the efficiency."

"Here are man's works, and here are God's works . . . With these two combined powers, man will be victorious. , . . He puts to the stretch every spiritual nerve and muscle that he may be a successful overcomer in his work, and that he may obtain the precious boon of eternal life."

DA 118: "For our sake He exercised a self-control stronger than hunger or death. And in this first victory were involved other issues that enter into all our conflicts with the powers of darkness."

KH 88 (L 66, 1898): "The Lord requires us to sink self in Jesus Christ, and let the glory be all of God."

SC 43: "The warfare against self is the greatest battle that was ever fought."

FE 195: "Terrible are the consequences of not having a **constant** connection with God."

AA 531: "God calls upon us to reach the standard of perfection, and places before us the example of Christ's character. In His humanity, **perfected by a life of constant resistance of evil, the**

48

Saviour showed that through cooperation with Divinity, human beings may in this life attain to perfection of character. This is God's assurance to us that we too may obtain complete victory."

DA 71: "Jesus was placed where His character would be tested. It was necessary for Him to be constantly on guard in order to preserve His purity. He was subject to all the conflicts which we have to meet, that He might be an example for us in childhood, youth, and manhood."

KH 16: "The Holy Spirit must be constantly imparted to man, or he has ho disposition to contend against the powers of darkness."

CG 483 (MS 140, 1897): "Every day of our lives we should surrender ourselves to God. Thus we may gain special help and daily victories. The cross is to be borne daily. Every word should be guarded, for we are responsible to God to represent in our lives as far as possible the character of Christ."

PP 248: "In order to receive God's help, man must realize his weakness and deficiency; he must apply his own mind to the great change to be wrought in himself; he must be aroused to earnest and persevering prayer and effort. Wrong habits and customs must be shaken off: and it is only by determined endeavor to correct these errors, and conform to right principles, that the victory can be gained. Many never attain to the position that they might occupy, because they wait for God to do for them that which He has given them power to do for themselves. All who are fitted for usefulness must be trained by the severest mental and moral discipline; and God will ASSIST them BY UNITING DIVINE POWER WITH HUMAN EFFORT."

FILB 135 (RH Dec. 16, 1884): "The evil tendencies of mankind are hard to overcome. The battles are tedious. Every soul in the strife knows how severe, how bitter, are these contests. Everything about growth in grace is difficult, because the standard maxims of the world are constantly interposed between the soul and God's holy standard. . . . We must gain the victory over self, crucify the affections and lusts; and then begins the union of the soul with Christ . . . After this union is formed, it can be preserved only by continual, earnest, painstaking effort.

"Every Christian must stand on guard continually, watching every avenue of the soul, where Satan might find access. He must pray for divine help and at the same time resolutely resist every inclination to sin. By courage, by faith, by persevering toil, he can conquer. But let him remember that to gain the victory Christ must abide in him and he in Christ. . . . It is only by personal union with Christ, by communion with Him daily, hourly, that we can bear the fruits of the Holy Spirit."

CHRIST WAS NOT TO CALL HIS DIVINITY
TO HIS AID

QOD 656 (RH Sept. 4, 1900): "He might have helped His human nature . . . by pouring forth from His divine nature . . . but He humbled Himself to man's nature."

DA 119: "And **Christ was not to exercise divine power for His own benefit,** He had come to bear trial as we must do, leaving us an example of faith and submission. Neither here nor at any subsequent time in His earthly life did He work a miracle in His own behalf."

RH July 28, 1874: "Christ in the wilderness of temptation, stood in Adam's place to bear the test he failed to endure."

DA 335: "But He rested **not** in possession of almighty power. It was **not** as the 'Master of earth and sea and sky' that He reposed in quiet. **That power He had laid down,** and He says, 'I can of mine own self do nothing.' He trusted to the Father's might. It was in faith — faith in God's love and care — that Jesus rested, and the power of that word which stilled the storm was the power of God."

Redemption, or the Sufferings of Christ, 16: "He must not call His divinity to His aid, but as a man, He must bear the consequences of man's sin and the Creator's displeasure toward His disobedient subjects. As He felt His unity with the Father broken up, He feared that his **human** nature would be unable to endure the coming conflict . . ."

THE DEATH STRUGGLE

NOTE: In Gethsemane and on the cross, the difficult temptation for Christ was to keep from reverting to His divine mind to aid Him in the final death struggle. But He must not do this or the plan of salvation would be a failure.

He could not have suffered the penalty for lost humanity which was eternal death and final separation from God.

The Son of God having made the sacrifice to become subject to the decision of the Divine will, the Son of Man must go through the death struggle alone. This price He paid, leaving the final decision with His Father as to when justice would be satisfied, and whether He should ever live again.

On the morning of the resurrection, Gabriel brings the summons from God, the judge Himself, that justice is satisfied: "Son of God Thy Father calls Thee." **Infinite life, laid down for a finite time, was more than an equivalent, for finite lives, for an infinite tme.**

DA 693: "The angel (Gabriel) came not to take the cup from Christ's hand, but to strengthen Him to drink it."

QOD 660 (2SP 11, 12): "The extent of the terrible consequences of sin could never have been known, had not the remedy been of **infinite** value."

NOTE: Thus the penalty was met, and salvation for lost men assured. O, marvelous condescension of a gracious God and Saviour!

DA 790: "He ascended the heavenly courts, and from God Himself heard the assurance that His atonement for the sins of men had been ample, that through His blood all might gain eternal life. The Father ratified the covenant made with Christ, that He would receive repentant and obedient men, and would love them even as He loves His Son."

PP 65: "But an angel's life could not pay the debt. Only He who created man had power to redeem him."

5BC 1113 (L 280, 1904): "When Christ was crucified, it was His human nature that died. Divinity did not sink and die; THAT WOULD HAVE BEEN IMPOSSIBLE."

QOD 650 (ST June 29, 1898): "Christ came to the earth, taking humanity and standing as man's representative, to show in the controversy with Satan, that man as God created him, **connected with the Father and the Son,** could obey every divine requirement."

1SM 252 (ST June 9, 1898): "After the fall of man, Satan declared that human beings were proved to be incapable of keeping the law of God, and he sought to carry the universe with him in this belief. Satan's words appeared to be true, and Christ came to unmask the deceiver. The Majesty of Heaven undertook the cause of man, and with the same facilities that man may obtain, withstood the temptations of Satan as man must withstand them. This was the only way in which fallen man could become a partaker of the divine nature."

FILB 114 (MS 48, 1893): "Christ came to the world to counteract Satan's falsehood that God had made a law which men could not keep. Taking humanity upon Himself, He came to this earth, and by a life of obedience showed that God has not made a law that man cannot keep. He showed that it is possible for man perfectly to obey the law. . . . Man is to show by his obedience that he could be trusted in heaven, that he would not rebel."

OHC 48 (MS 1, 1892): "The obedience of Christ to His Father was the same obedience that is required of **MAN** . . . The Lord Jesus came to our world, not to reveal what a God could do, but what a man could do, through faith in God's power to help in every emergency . . . the world's Redeemer, could only keep the commandments of God in the same way that humanity can keep them."

7BC 930 (MS 1, 1892): "If Christ had a special power which it is not the privilege of man to have, Satan would have made capital of this matter. The work of Christ was to take from the claims of Satan his control of man, and he could do this only in the way that He came — a man, tempted as a man, rendering the obedience of a man."

7BC 929 (MS 1, 1892): ". . . We make many mistakes because of our erroneous views of the human nature of our Lord. When we give to His human nature a power that it is not possible for man to have in his conflicts with Satan, we destroy the completeness of His humanity. His imputed grace and power He gives to all who receive Him by faith."

PP 154-155: "Because Abraham had shown a lack of faith in God's promises, Satan had accused him before the angels and before God of having failed to comply with the conditions of the covenant, and as unworthy of its blessings. God desired to prove the loyalty of His servant before all heaven, to demonstrate that nothing less than perfect obedience can be accepted, and to open more fully before them the plan of salvation."

ST June 17, 1897: "**Had He not been fully human, Christ could not have been our substitute.** He could not have worked out in humanity that perfection of character which it is the privilege of all to reach. . . . **In His humanity, He laid hold of the divinity of God; and this every member** of the human family has the privilege of doing. **Christ did nothing that human nature may not do if it partakes of the divine nature."**

1SM 286 (RH Sept. 1, 1874): "The eye of Jesus for a moment rested upon the glory presented before Him; but He turned away and refused to look upon the entrancing spectacle. He would not endanger His steadfast integrity by dallying with the tempter. When Satan solicited homage, Christ's divine indignation was aroused, and He could no longer tolerate the blasphemous assumption of Satan, or even permit him to remain in His presence. Here Christ exercised His divine authority, and commanded Satan to desist. 'Get thee hence, Satan, . . . ' "

QOD 650 (YI June 2, 1889): "Christ is called the second Adam. He began where the first Adam began. Willingly He passed over the ground where Adam fell, and redeemed Adam's failure."

RH March 26, 1901: "He was God in human flesh, and He could not but work the works of God. Unbelief, prejudice, and jealousy beat about Him, and if His humanity had not been united with divinity, He would have failed and become discouraged. At times His divinity flashed through humanity. and He stood forth as the Son of God. His veil of flesh too transparent to hide His majesty."

PP 421: "Exercise self-control under the greatest provocation."

THE RIGHTEOUSNESS OF THE HUMAN CHRIST

ST May 10, 1899: "**Satan had asserted that man could not keep the commandments of God. To prove that they could Christ became a man, and lived the life of perfect obedience . . . through divine power."**

1SP 49: "**Satan hoped . . . that He (Christ) would manifest His divine power . . . and thus the plan of salvation at last fail."**

Redemption or The Sufferings of Christ 59: "Satan instigated the cruel abuse of the debased mob, led on by the priests and rulers to **PROVOKE, IF POSSIBLE, RETALIATION** from the world's Redeemer, **OR** TO DRIVE HIM TO DELIVER HIMSELF BY A MIRACLE from the hands of His persecutors AND **THUS BREAK UP THE PLAN OF SALVATION.** One stain upon His **HUMAN** life, one failure of His **HUMANITY** to bear the terrible test imposed upon it, would make the Lamb of God an imperfect offering **AND THE REDEMPTION OF MAN WOULD BE A FAILURE."**

Note: With every conceivable insult in an attempt to force Him to retaliate and lose His composure and self-mastery, He was "pushed," "shoved," "dragged," "slapped," "spit" upon, but all to no avail, and finally they crucified Him. **He maintained self-mastery to the end. This is the goal for all overcomers who expect translation.** "It is the issue of the daily test that determines their victory or defeat in life's great crisis." DA, 382.

THE HUMAN CHRIST WAS FITTED FOR THE DAILY

CONFLICT BY THE INDWELLING OF THE HOLY SPIRIT

DA 123: " 'The prince of this world cometh' saith Jesus, 'and hath nothing in Me." There was nothing in Him that responded to Satan's sophistry. He did not consent to sin. **Not even by a thought did He yield to temptation. So it may be with us.** Christ's humanity was united with divinity; **He was fitted for the conflict by the indwelling of the Holy Spirit.** And He came to make us partakers of the divine nature. So long as we are united to Him by faith, sin has no more dominion over us. God reaches for the hand of faith in us to direct it to lay fast hold upon the divinity of Christ, that we may attain to perfection of character."

A Solemn Appeal. 29; "If Satan seeks to divert the mind from this to low and sensual things, bring it back again, and place it on eternal things; when the Lord **sees the determined effort made to retain only pure thoughts, He will attract the mind, like the magnet,** and purify the thoughts, and enable them to cleanse themselves from every secret sin."

MH 453-454: "There is a science of Christianity to be mastered, — a science as much deeper, broader, higher than any human science as the heavens are higher than the earth. The mind is to be disciplined, educated, trained; for we are to do service for God in ways that are not in harmony with inborn inclination. **Hereditary and cultivated tendencies to evil must be overcome. Often the education and training of a lifetime must be discarded, that one may become a learner in the school of Christ. Our hearts must be educated to become steadfast in God. We are to form habits of thought that will enable us to resist temptation."**

RH March 27, 1888: "There are thoughts and feelings suggested and aroused by Satan that annoy even the best of men; but if they are not cherished, if they are repulsed as hateful, the soul is not contaminated with guilt and no other is defiled by their influence."

RH Jan. 18, 1909: "Christ in the weakness of humanity was to meet the temptations of one possessing the power of the higher nature that God had bestowed upon the angelic family. But Christ's humanity was united with divinity, and in this strength He would bear all the temptations that Satan could bring against Him, and yet keep His soul untainted by sin. **And this power to overcome, He would give to every son and daughter of Adam who would accept by faith the righteous attributes of His character.** God loved the world so dearly that He gave His only begotten Son, that **whosoever** would accept Him might have power to live His sinless life."

OHC 265 (MS 60, 1894): "It is our duty to train and discipline the body . . . We are not to pamper the appetite . . . The sacred temple of the body must be kept pure and uncontaminated, that God's Holy Spirit may dwell therein."

KH 16 (RH July 18, 1882): "The Holy Spirit must be constantly imparted to man, or he has no disposition to contend against the powers of darkness."

DA 671: "The Spirit was to be given as a regenerating agent, and without this the sacrifice of Christ would have been of no avail. Sin could be resisted and overcome only through the mighty agency of the third person of the Godhead who would come with no modified energy, but in the fullness of divine power. It is the Spirit that makes effectual what has been wrought out by the world's Redeemer. It is by the Spirit that the heart is made pure. Through the Spirit the believer becomes a partaker of the divine nature. Christ has given His Spirit as a divine power to overcome all hereditary and cultivated tendencies to evil, and to impress His own character upon His church."

AA 482: "The work of gaining salvation is one of co-partnership, a joint operation. There is to be cooperation between God and the repentant sinner. This is necessary for the formation of right principles in the character. Man is to make earnest efforts to overcome that which hinders him from attaining to perfection. But he is wholly dependent upon God for success. Human effort of itself is not sufficient. Without the aid of divine power, it avails nothing. God works and man works. Resistance of temptation must come from man, who must draw his power from God."

THE RELATION OF THE HOLY SPIRIT
TO HUMAN EFFORT

TM 518: "As fast as the soul resolves to act . . . the Holy Spirit gives . . . strength. . . . The Spirit is supplied to co-operate with the soul's resolve."

1T 619: "I was shown that if God's people make no efforts on their part, but wait for the refreshing to come upon them and remove their wrongs and correct their errors; if they depend upon that to cleanse them from filthiness of the flesh and spirit, and fit them to engage in the loud cry of the third angel, they will be found wanting. The refreshing or power of God comes only on those who have prepared themselves for it by doing the work which God bids them, namely, cleansing themselves from all filthiness of the flesh and spirit, perfecting holiness in the fear of God.

1SM 380 (MS 26a, 1892): "His power awaits the demand of those who would overcome."

1SM 411 (RH Feb. 18, 1890): "If divine power does not combine with human effort, I would not give a straw for all that the greatest man could do."

FILB 165 (Sp T, A. 9, p. 58, 1896): "A great lesson is learned when we understand our relation to God, and His relation to us."

1SM 382 (ST June 16, 1890): "When it is in the heart to obey God, when efforts are put forth to this end, Jesus accepts this disposition and effort as man's best service, and He makes up for the deficiency with His own divine merit. But He will not accept those who claim to have faith in Him, and yet are disloyal to His Father's commandment. We hear a great deal about faith, but we need to hear a great deal more about works. Many are deceiving their own souls by living an easygoing, accommodating, crossless religion. But Jesus says, 'If any man will come after me, let him deny himself, and take up his cross, and follow me.' "

RH Nov. 22, 1892: "Man is privileged to connect with Christ, and then the divine and the human combine; and in this union the hope of man must rest alone; for it is as the Spirit of God touches the soul that the powers of the soul are quickened, and man becomes a new creature in Christ Jesus."

NBL. The Church, No. 5, 3: "Unless the Holy Spirit works upon the human heart at every step, we shall stumble and fall."

RH Nov. 29, 1892: "The work of the Holy Spirit is **immeasurably great** . . . the personal presence of Christ in the soul."

OHC 153 (RH Aug. 25, 1896): ". . . the human will must be blended with the divine. This will bring the Holy Spirit to our aid."

KH 16 (RH July 18, 1882): "The Holy Spirit must be constantly imparted to man, or he has no disposition to contend against the powers of darkness."

Letter Oct. 10, 1899: "One little disregard of 'thus saith the Lord' is sufficient to stop the promised blessing of the Holy Spirit."

DA 693: "The angel (Gabriel) came not to take the cup from Christ's hand, but to strengthen Him to drink it."

AA 51: "The Spirit furnishes the strength that sustains striving, wrestling souls in every emergency."

OHC 48 (7BC 929, MS 1, 1892): "The obedience of Christ to His Father was the same obedience that is required of MAN . . . The Lord Jesus came to our world, not to reveal what a God could do, but what a man could do, through faith in God's power to help in every emergency . . . the world's Redeemer, could only keep the commandments of God in the same way that humanity can keep them."

OHC 91 (L 135, 1898): "And it is the very hardest, sternest conflict which comes with the purpose and hour of great resolve and decision of the human to incline the will and way to God's will and God's way. Man is allotted a part in this great struggle for everlasting life; . . . It will require a struggle to break through the powers of darkness, but the Spirit that works in him can and will accomplish this. But man is no passive instrument to be saved in indolence. He is called upon to strain every muscle in the struggle for immortality; yet it is God that supplies the efficiency."

"Here are man's works, and here are God's works . . . With these two combined powers, man will be victorious, . . . He puts to the stretch every spiritual nerve and muscle that he may be a successful overcomer in his work, and that he may obtain the precious boon of eternal life."

RH June 11, 1901: "If we are faithful in **doing our part, in cooperating with Him,** God will work through us to do the good pleasure of His will, **but cannot work through us if we make no effort.** If we gain eternal life, we must work, and work earnestly. . . . **Our part is to put away sin, seek with determination for perfection of character. As we thus work, God cooperates with us.** . . . Let us not be deceived by the oft-repeated assertion, 'all we have to do is believe.' **Faith and works are two oars which we must use equally** if we would press our way up the stream. . . . **'Faith,** if it hath not works, is dead, being alone.' The Christian is a man of thought and practice. His faith fixes its roots firmly in Christ. **By faith** and **good works** he keeps his spirituality strong and healthy, and his spiritual strength increases **as he strives** to work the works of God."

PP 248: "In order to receive God's help, man must realize his weakness and deficiency; he must apply his own mind to the great change to be wrought in himself; he must be aroused to earnest and persevering prayer and effort. **Wrong habits and customs must be shaken off:** and it is only by determined endeavor to correct these errors, and conform to right principles, that the victory can be gained. Many never attain to the position that they might occupy, because they wait for God to do for them that which He has given them power to do for themselves. All who are fitted for usefulness must be trained by the severest mental and moral discipline; and God will **assist** them **by uniting divine power with human effort.**"

AA 531: "God calls upon us to reach the standard of perfection, and places before us the example of Christ's character. **In His humanity, perfected by a life of constant resistance of evil, the Saviour showed that through cooperation with divinity human beings may in this life attain to perfection of character.** This is God's assurance to us that we too may obtain complete victory."

MH 452: "The struggle for conquest over self, for holiness and heaven, is a life-long struggle. Without continual effort and constant activity, there can be no advancement in the divine life, no attainment of the victors crown."

PP 73: "Without the works of obedience faith is dead."

GC 472: "The testimony of the word of God is against this ensnaring doctrine of faith without works. It is not faith that claims the favor of heaven without complying with the conditions upon which mercy is to be granted, it is presumption; for genuine faith has its foundation in the promise and provisions of the Scriptures."

TM 240: "The Lord does not propose to perform for us either the willing or the doing. This is our proper work. As soon as we earnestly enter upon the work, God's grace is given to work in us to will and to do, but never as a substitute for our effort. Our souls are to be aroused to cooperate. The Holy Spirit works the human agent, to work out our own salvation. This is the practical lesson the Holy Spirit is striving to teach us."

OHC 310 (L 135, 1897): "Man cannot be towed to heaven; he cannot go as a passive passenger. He must himself use the oars, and work as a laborer together with God . . .

"It is only by earnest effort, by using the oars with all your might, that you can stem the current. How many there are as weak as water . . . God will help us if we take hold of the help He has provided. . . . There are two grand forces at work in the salvation of the human soul. It requires the cooperation of man with God."

2SM 381 (L Dec. 8, 1886): "I do not mean that cheap faith unsupported by works, but that earnest, living, constant, abiding faith, that eats the flesh and drinks the blood of the Son of God."

GC 487: "Only the love which is shown by works is counted genuine."

NBL. Vol. 1. A Work of Cooperation. Education, No. 4. Vol. 1. No. 28: "We may all strive for perfection of character, but all who come into possession of it will earn it step by step, by the cultivation of the virtues which God commends."

5T 472: "We are to exert every energy of the soul in the work of overcoming, and to look to Jesus for strength to do what we cannot do of ourselves."

RH Jan. 24, 1893: "Some will not make a right use of the doctrine of justification by faith. They will present it in a **ONE-SIDED** manner, making everything of faith and belittling works. Others will seize the points that have a leaning toward error, and will ignore works altogether. Now genuine faith always works by love; it supplies a motive power. Faith is **not an opiate, but a stimulant.** . . . Looking to Calvary will not quiet your soul into non-performance of duty, but will create faith that will work, purifying the soul from all selfishness. In laying hold of Christ by faith, we but just begin our work. Every man has corrupt and sinful habits, that must be overcome through vigorous warfare. Every soul must fight the fight of faith."

RH Jan. 24, 1893: The servant of God gives us a warning against **Satan's attempt to confuse minds regarding the "right use of the doctrine of justification by faith**. . . . He (Satan) will work with his masterly power to bring **fanaticism** on one hand and cold **formalism** on the other, **that he may gather in a harvset of souls.** Now is the time to watch unceasingly. Watch for the first steps of advance that Satan may make against us. There are dangers to be guarded against on the right hand and on the left. Some will not make a right use of the doctrine of justification by faith, they will present it in a **one-sided manner,** making everything of faith and belittling works."

KH 229 (ST June 16, 1890): "The faith we are required to have is not a do-nothing faith; saving faith is that which works by love and purifies the soul . . . Faith· and works will keep us evenly balanced, and make us successful in the work of. perfecting Christian character."

GC 487: "Only the love which is shown by works is counted genuine."

PP 73: "Without the works of obedience faith is dead."

RH April 11, 1880: "The pleasing fable that all there is to do is to believe, has destroyed thousands and tens of thousands, because many have called that faith which is not faith, but simply a dogma. Man is an intelligent, accountable, being. He is not to be carried as a passive burden by the Lord, but is to work in harmony with Christ. Man is to take up his appointed work in striving for glory, honor and immortality. God calls upon man for the use of every talent He has lent them, the exercise of every power He has given them: for man can never be saved in disobedience and indolence."

RH Nov. 4, 1890: "No man can cover his soul with the garment of Christ's righteousness while practicing known sins, or neglecting known duties. God requires the entire surrender of the heart, before justification can take place; and in order for man to retain justification, there must be continual obedience, through active living faith that works by love and purifies the soul."

RH Sept. 3, 1889: "The doctrine of justification by faith has been lost sight of by many who have professed to believe the third angel's message. There is not one in one hundred who understands for himself the Bible truth on this subject that is so necessary to our present and eternal welfare."

6T 19: "The message of Christ's righteousness is to sound from one end of the earth to the other to prepare the way of the Lord. This is the glory of God which closes the work of the third angel."

RH April 1, 1890: "Several have written to me, inquiring if the message of justification by faith is the third angel's message, and I have answered, it is the third angel's message in verity."

DA 49: "He permitted Him to meet life's peril in common with every human soul, to fight the battle as every child of humanity must fight it, at the risk of failure and eternal loss."

SC 50: "The poor sufferer was helpless; he had not used his limbs for thirty-eight years. Yet Jesus bade him 'rise, take up thy bed, and walk.' The sick man might have said, 'Lord, if Thou wilt make me whole, I will obey Thy word.' But no, he believed Christ's word, believed that he was made whole, and he made the effort at once; he willed to walk, and he did walk. **He acted on the word of Christ, and God gave the power.** He was made whole."

MYP 55 (RH Feb. 10, 1903): "Our finite **will** must be brought into submission to the **will** of the Divine; the human **will must be blended** with the Divine. This will bring the Holy Spirit to our aid."

MM 12 (K 205, 1899): "The sick are to be healed through the combined efforts of the human and the divine."

MM 12 (RH Jan. 14, 1902): "Sin brings physical and spiritual disease and weakness, Christ has made it possible for us to free ourselves of this curse. The Lord promises by the medium of truth to renovate the soul. The Holy Spirit will make all who are willing to be educated, able to communicate the truth with power. It will renew every organ of the body, that God's servants may work acceptably and successfully. Vitality increases under the influence of the Spirit's action. Let us by this power lift ourselves into a higher, holier atmosphere, that we may do well our appointed work."

KH 88 (L 66, 1898): "The Lord requires us to sink self in Jesus Christ, and let the glory be all of God."

SC 43: "God desires to heal us, to set us free. But since this requires an entire transformation, a renewing of our whole nature, we must yield ourselves wholly to Him."

THE PURPOSE OF CHRIST IN OUR HUMAN NATURE WAS TO SET A PATTERN FOR THE CONVERTED OR BORN-AGAIN MAN, SHOWING HIM HOW TO OBTAIN VICTORY OVER THE FLESH, THE DEVIL, AND THE WORLD

YI Oct. 20, 1886: ". . . (He) became like one of us except in sin, that **His life** and character should be **a pattern for all to copy. . . ."**

9T 22: "The life that Christ lived in this world, men and women can live, through His power and under His instruction. In their conflict with Satan, they may have all the help that He had. They may be more than conquerors through Him who loved them and gave Himself for them."

OHC 99 (L 186, 1902): ". . . He (Christ) must be exemplified in the minutest details of everyday service . . ."

OHC 99 (MS 6, 1906): "As Christ the pattern is constantly put before the minds eye, new habits will be formed, powerful hereditary and cultivated tendencies will be subdued and overcome, self-esteem will be laid in the dust, old habits of thought will be constantly resisted, love for the supremacy will be seen in its real, despicable character, and will be overcome."

2T 549: "He is a perfect and holy example given for us to imitate. We cannot equal the pattern; but we shall not be approved of God if we do not copy it and, according to the ability which God has given, resemble it."

QOD 658 (YI June 2, 1898): "In His human nature He maintained the purity of His divine character."

DA 24: "As one of us, He gave an **example** of **obedience.** For this **He took upon Himself our nature, and passed through our experiences.** In all things it **behooved Him to be made like unto His brethren.** If we had to bear anything which Jesus did not endure, then upon this point Satan would represent the power of God as insufficient for us. Therefore Jesus was 'in all points tempted like as we are.' He endured every trial to which we are subject. And **He exercised in His own behalf no power that is not freely offered to us. As man** He met temptation and overcame in the strength given Him from God."

GC 510: "Satan assailed Christ with his fiercest and most subtle temptations; but he was repulsed in every conflict. Those battles were fought in our behalf; those victories make it possible for us to conquer. Christ will give strength to all who seek it. . . . The fact that Christ has conquered should inspire His followers with courage to fight manfully the battle against sin and Satan."

RH May 16, 1907: "The same devotion, the same self- sacrifice, the same subjection to the claims of the word of God, that are manifest in the life of Christ, must be seen in the lives of His servants."

7BC 929 (MS 1, 1892): ". . . We make many mistakes because of our erroneous views of the human nature of our Lord. When we give to His human nature a power that it is not possible for man to have in his conflicts with Satan, we destroy the completeness of His humanity. His imputed grace and power He gives to all who receive Him by faith."

Redemption, or The Ascension of Christ, 77: "It was His difficult task to maintain **the level of humanity.**"

RH April 1, 1875: "Christ was put to the test requiring the strength of all His faculties to resist the inclination when in danger, to use His power to deliver Himself from peril and triumph over the power of the prince of darkness. It was as difficult for Him to keep the level of humanity as it was for men to rise above the level of their depraved natures and be partakers of the divine nature."

QOD 651 (YI April 25, 1901): "The enemy was overcome by Christ in His human nature."

Redemption, or the Ascension of Christ 78: "He had wrought out a **righteous** character on earth as an **example for man to follow.**"

AA 531: "God calls upon us to reach the standard of perfection, and places before us the example of Christ's character. **In His humanity, perfected by a life of constant resistance of evil, the Saviour showed that through cooperation with divinity human beings may in this life attain to perfection of character.** This is God's assurance to us that we too may obtain complete victory."

MH 181: The Saviour overcame to show man how he may overcome."

RH Feb. 18, 1890: "Christ came to reveal the source of His power, that man might never rely on his **unaided** capabilities. Those who would overcome must put to the tax every power of their being. They must agonize on their knees before God for divine power."

1T 144: "We can overcome. Yes; fully, entirely. Jesus died to make a way of escape for us, that we might overcome every evil temper, every sin, every temptation, and sit down at last with Him."

5T 472: "We are to exert every energy of the soul in the work of overcoming, and to look to Jesus for strength to do what we cannot do of ourselves."

7BC 974 (L 236, 1908): "We become overcomers by helping others to overcome, by the blood of the Lamb and the word of our testimony."

PK 637: "He (Nehemiah) united his petitions with holy endeavor, putting forth earnest prayerful efforts for the success of the enterprise in which he was engaged."

KH 34 (RH Nov. 8, 1887): "We must look to Christ; we must resist as He resisted; we must pray as he prayed; we must agonize as He agonized, if we would conquer as He conquered."

COL 82: "We have a part to act, but we must have the power of divinity to unite with us, or our efforts will be in vain."

SM 380 (MS 26a, 1892): "His power awaits the demand of those who would overcome."

1SM 411 (RH Feb. 18, 1890): "If divine power does not combine with human effort, I would not give a straw for all that the greatest man could do."

4T 32-33: "Man must work with his human power aided by the divine power of Christ, to resist and conquer at any cost to himself. In short, man must overcome as Christ overcame. . . . This could not be the case if Christ alone did all the overcoming. **Man must be victor on his own account.**"

5BC 1062 (RH Feb. 18, 1890): "Men may have a power to resist evil — a power that neither earth, nor death nor hell can master; a power that will place them where they may overcome as Christ overcame. Divinity and humanity may be combined in them."

RH June 29, 1897: "The Holy Spirit is the source of all power, and works as a living, active agent in the new life created in the soul. The Holy Spirit is to be in us a divine indweller."

MYP 165 (YI July 27, 1889): "He (Jesus) came to show man **how** to obey, **how** to keep all the commandments. **He laid hold of divine power, and this is the sinner's only hope.**"

DA 363: "As a man He supplicated the throne of God till His humanity was charged with a heavenly current that should connect humanity with divinity. Through continual communion He received life from God that He might impart life to the world. His experience is to be ours."

ST June 17, 1897: "Had He not been fully human, Christ could not have been our substitute. He could not have worked out in humanity that perfection of character which it is the privilege of all to reach. . . . In His humanity, He laid hold of the divinity of God; and this every member of the human family has the privilege of doing. Christ did nothing that human nature may not do if it partakes of the divine nature."

2T 355: "We believe without a doubt that Christ is soon coming. . . . When He comes He is not to cleanse us of our sins, to remove from us the defects in our characters, or to cure us of the infirmities of our tempers and dispositions. If wrought for us at all, this work will all be accomplished before that time. When the Lord comes, those who are holy will be holy still. Those who have preserved their bodies and spirits in holines, in sanctification and honor, will then receive the finishing touch of immortality."

5BC 1085 (MS 34, 1899): "The Lord requires perfection from His redeemed family. He calls for perfection in character building."

PP 509: "The secret of success is the union of divine power with human effort."

MB 117-118: "He (God) tells us to be perfect as He is — in the same manner. We are to be centers of light and blessing in our circle, even as He is to the universe . . . We may be perfect in our sphere, even as God is perfect in His."

GC 620: "Those who delay a preparation for the day of God cannot obtain it in the time of trouble, or at any subsequent time. **The case of all such is hopeless.**"

AA 531: "God calls upon us to reach the standard of perfection, and places before us the example of Christ's character. **In His humanity, perfected by a life of constant resistance of evil, the Saviour showed that through co-operation with divinity human beings may in this life at-**

tain to perfection of character. This is God's assurance to us that we too may obtain complete victory."

CG 477 (MS 19, 1900): "He calls upon you to cooperate with Him in teaching them to form perfect characters. The Lord requires prefection from His redeemed family. He expects from us the perfection which Christ revealed in His humanity."

KH 34 (RH Nov. 8, 1887): "We must look to Christ; we must resist as He resisted; we must pray as he prayed; we must agonize as He agonized, if we would conquer as He conquered."

DF 153 (CTBH 16, 1890): "His (Christ's) victory is an assurance that we too may come off victors in our conflicts with the enemy. But it is not our heavenly Father's purpose to save us without an effort on our part to cooperate with Christ. We must act our part, and divine power, uniting with our effort will bring victory."

DA 668: "And if we consent, He will so identify Himself with our thoughts and aims, so blend our hearts and minds into conformity to His will, that when obeying Him we shall be but carrying out our own impulses."

GC 510: "Satan assailed Christ with his fiercest and most subtile temptations; but he was repulsed in every conflict. Those battles were fought in our behalf; those victories make it possible for us to conquer. Christ will give strength to all who seek it. . . . The fact that Christ has conquered should inspire His followers with courage to fight manfully the battle against sin and Satan."

2T 355: "We believe without a doubt that Christ is soon coming. . . . When He comes He is not to cleanse us of our sins, to remove from us the defects in our characters, or to cure us of the infirmities of our tempers and dispositions. If wrought for us at all, this work will all be accomplished before that time. When the Lord comes, those who are holy will be holy still. Those who have preserved their bodies and spirits in holiness, in sanctification and honor, will then receive the finishing touch of immortality."

DA 71: "Jesus was placed where His character would be tested. **It was necessary for Him to be constantly on guard in order to preserve His purity.** He was subject to all the conflicts which we have to meet, that He might be an example for us in childhood, youth, and manhood."

KH 16 (RH July 18, 1882): "The Holy Spirit must be constantly imparted to man, or he has no disposition to contend against the powers of darkness."

FE 195: "Terrible are the consequences of not having a **constant** connection with God."

Gal. 5:7: "For the flesh lusteth against the Spirit, and the Spirit against the flesh . . . "

Rom. 6:11: ". . . **Reckon** ye also yourselves to be dead indeed unto sin, but alive unto God . . ."

AS CHRIST, BY THE INDWELLING OF THE HOLY SPIRIT CONDEMNED SIN IN HIS FLESH, SO WE BY THE INDWELLING OF THE HOLY SPIRIT ARE TO CONDEMN SIN IN OUR FLESH

Romans 8:3, 4, 12, 13: "For what the law could not do, in that it was weak through the flesh, God, sending his own Son in the **likeness of sinful flesh,** and for sin, **condemned sin in the flesh: That the righteousness of the law might be fulfilled in us, who walk not after the flesh, but after the Spirit.** Therefore, brethren, we are debtors, not to the flesh, to live after the flesh. For if ye live after the flesh, ye shall die: **but if ye through the Spirit do mortify the deeds of the body, ye shall live."**

A SINLESS CHRIST

5BC 1128: "Be careful, exceedingly careful, how you dwell upon the human nature of Christ. Do not set Him before the people as a man with propensities of sin. He is the second Adam. The first Adam was created a pure, sinless being, without a taint of sin upon him.** He was made in the image of God. . . . **But Jesus Christ took upon Himself human nature,** and was tempted in all points as human nature is tempted. He could have sinned: He could have fallen, but **not for one moment was there in Him an evil propensity. He was assailed with temptations in the wilderness as Adam was assailed with temptations in Eden."**

DA 664: "His perfect humanity is that which all His followers may possess, if they will be in subjection to God as He was."

RH July 28, 1874: "Christ bore the sins and infirmities of the race as they existed when He came to the earth to help man. In behalf of the race, **with the weaknesss of fallen man upon Him,** He was to stand the temptation of Satan upon all points wherewith man would be assailed."

DA 117: "In our humanity Christ was to redeem Adam's failure. But when Adam was assailed by the tempter, none of the effects of sin were upon him. . . . It was not thus with Jesus when He entered the wilderness to cope with Satan. For four thousand years the race had been decreasing in physical strength, in mental power, and in moral worth; and **Christ took upon Him the infirmities of degenerate humanity. Only thus could He rescue man** from the lowest depths of his degradation. Many claim that it was impossible for Christ to be overcome by temptation. Then He could not have been placed in Adam's position; He could not have gained the victory that Adam failed to gain. If we have in any sense a more trying conflict than had Christ, then He would not be able to succor us. But our Saviour took humanity, with all its liabilities. He took the nature of man, with the possibility of yielding to temptation. We have nothing to bear which He has not endured."

RH Feb. 18, 1904: "I must overcome the temptations that surround me, else they will drive Christ from my heart. He combats all temptation and braves all opposition. By the strength obtained from on high, he holds in control the passions and tendencies which uncontrolled, would lead him to defeat."

Special Instruction Relating to the R & H Office, and the Work of Battle Creek, 13, May 26, 1896: "Though He had no taint of sin. . . . **having taken our fallen nature, He showed what it might become.**"

DA 48: "He came to **give us an example of a sinless life.**"

5T 422: **"Not a single thought or feeling responded to temptation.**

MH 157: "Of all the people in the world, reformers should be the most unselfish, the most kind, the most courteous."

RH March 16, 1886: "Do not wait for a strong impulse before you move. If I had waited for feeling, one half of my life would have been spent without doing anything. Feeling is not to be our criterion.

2T 201-202: "He is a brother in our infirmities, but not in possessing like passions. As the sinless One His nature **recoiled** from evil."

WHEN DOES TEMPTATION BECOME SIN?

4T 623: "When impure thoughts are **cherished,** they need not be expressed by word or act to consummate the sin and bring the soul into condemnation. Its purity is defiled, and the tempter has triumphed. . . **It is Satan's act to tempt you, but your own act to yield.** It is not in the power of all the hosts of Satan to force the tempted to transgress. There is no excuse for sin."

RH March 27, 1888: "There are thoughts and feelings suggested and aroused by Satan that annoy even the best of men; but if they are not cherished, if they are repulsed as hateful, the soul is not contaminated with guilt and no other is defiled by their influence."

YI July 20, 1899: "Temptation is resisted when a man is powerfully influenced to do a wrong action and, knowing that he can do it, resists by faith, with a firm hold upon divine power. This was the ordeal through which Christ passed."

5T 176-177: "The sin of evil speaking begins with the cherishing of evil thoughts. Guile includes impurity in all its forms. An impure thought **tolerated,** an unholy desire **cherished,** and the soul is contaminated, its integrity compromised. . . . If we would not commit sin, we must shun its very beginnings. Every emotion and desire must be held in subjection to reason and conscience. **Every unholy thought must be instantly repelled.** . . . No man can be forced to transgress. His own consent must be first gained; **the soul must purpose the sinful act, before passion can dominate over reason,** or iniquity triumph over conscience. Temptation, however strong, is never an excuse for sin."

NOTE: The human Christ, born of the Holy Spirit of God and tabernacled in sinful human flesh, rejected, repulsed, condemned the same without receiving a single taint of sin, and thus demonstrated for all who would be converted (born again) that they too could live a victorious, sinless life.

No temptation was permitted to register in His mind. He repulsed it instantly, as we may do. Thus, He did not have like passions as we have because He did not let them rise in His being. If the spirit of God dwells in us, we too may have this mastery.

2T 265: "The mind must be educated and disciplined to love purity."

2T 201-202: "He is a brother in our infirmities, but not in possessing like passions. As the sinless One His nature recoiled from evil."

RH Feb. 18, 1904: "I must overcome the temptations that surround me, else they will drive Christ from my heart. He combats all temptation and braves all opposition. By the strength obtained from on high, he holds in control the passions and tendencies which uncontrolled, would lead him to defeat."

OHC 153 (RH Aug. 25, 1896): "When Satan is permitted to mold the will, he uses it to accomplish his ends . . . he stirs up the evil propensities, awakening unholy passions and ambitions."

EW 43: "I saw a covering that God was drawing over His people to protect them in the time of trouble; and every soul that was decided on the truth, **and was pure in heart,** was to be covered with the covering of the Almighty."

DA 312: "He took our nature and overcame, that we through taking His nature, might overcome. 'Made in the likeness of sinful flesh,' **He lived a sinless life."**

RH Jan. 28, 1909: "Christ in the weakness of humanity was to meet the temptations of one possessing the power of the higher nature that God had bestowed upon the angelic family. But Christ's humanity was united with divinity, and in this strength He would bear all the temptations that Satan could bring against Him, and yet keep His soul untainted by sin. **And this power to overcome, He would give to every son and daughter of Adam who would accept by faith the righteous atttributes of His character.** God loved the world so dearly that He gave His only begotten Son, that **whosoever would accept Him might have power to live His sinless life."**

DA 123: " 'The prince of this world cometh' said Jesus, 'and hath nothing in Me.' There was nothing in Him that responded to Satan's sophistry. He did not consent to sin. **Not even by a thought did He yield to temptation. So it may be with us.** Christ's humanity was united with divinity; **He was fitted for the conflict by the indwelling of the Holy Spirit.** And He came to make us partakers of the divine nature. So long as we are united to Him by faith, sin has no more dominion over us. God reaches for the hand of faith in us to direct it to lay fast hold upon the divinity of Christ, that we may attain to perfection of character."

9T 22: "The life that Christ lived in this world, men and women can live, through His power and under His instruction."

COL 388: "He seeks to develop in us the attributes of His character — compassion, tenderness and love."

A Solemn Appeal, 29: "If Satan seeks to divert the mind from this to low and sensual things, bring it back again, and place it on eternal things; and when the Lord **sees the determined effort made to retain only pure thoughts, He will attract the mind, like the magnet,** and purify the thoughts, and enable them to cleanse themselves from every secret sin."

FILB 316 (RH April 6, 1886): "The loins of the mind should be girded up, and the thoughts be trained to keep to the point, as the compass to the pole. . . . Worthy purposes should be kept constantly in view, and every thought and act should tend to their accomplishment. Let there ever be a fixedness of purpose to carry out that which is undertaken."

Sanctified Life, 67: "**If the mind wanders,** we must **bring it back;** by persevering effort, habit will finally make it easy."

2T 188: "Some need to discipline the mind by exercise. They should force it to think . . . Efforts must be made by every individual to educate the mind."

OHC 278 (RH Sept. 1, 1885): "Enoch's life and character, which was so holy that he was translated to heaven without seeing death, represents what the lives and characters of all must be, if, like Enoch, they are to be translated when Christ shall come."

RH Feb. 11, 1890: "Christ is cleansing the temple in heaven from the sins of the people, and we must work in harmony with Him upon the earth, cleansing the soul temple from its moral defilement."

1T 619: "I was shown that if God's people make no efforts on their part, but wait for the refreshing to come upon them and remove their wrongs and correct their errors; if they depend upon that to cleanse them from filthiness of the flesh and spirit, and fit them to engage in the loud cry of the third angel, they will be found wanting. The refreshing or power of God comes only on those who have prepared themselves for it by doing the work which God bids them, namely, cleansing themselves from all filthiness of the flesh and spirit, perfecting holiness in the fear of God."

DA 117. "In our humanity, Christ was to redeem Adam's failure. But when Adam was assailed by the tempter, none of the effects of sin were upon him. . . . It was not thus with Jesus when He entered the wilderness to cope with Satan. For four thousand years the race had been decreasing in physical strength, in mental power, and in moral worth; and **Christ took upon Him the infirmities of degenerate humanity. Only thus could He rescue man** from the lowest depths of his degradation. Many claim that it was impossible for Christ to be overcome by temptation. Then He could not have been placed in Adam's position; He could not have gained the victory that Adam failed to gain. If we have in any sense a more trying conflict than had Christ, then He would not be able to succor us. But our Saviour took humanity, with all its liabilities. He took the nature of man, with the possibility of yielding to temptation. We have nothing to bear which He has not endured."

1SM, 47: "Many a man professes to accept the testimonies, while they have no influence upon his life and character. His faults become stronger by indulgence until, having been often reproved and not heeding the reproof, he loses the power of self-control, and becomes hardened in a course of wrongdoing. If he is overworked, if weakness comes upon him, he has not moral power to rise above the infirmities of character which he did not overcome; they become his strongest points, and he is overborne by them."

COL 270: "When the voice of God awakens the dead, he will come forth with the same appetites and passions, the same likes and dislikes that he cherished when living. God works no miracle to re-create a man who would not be re-created when he was granted every opportunity and provided with every facility."

ST, July 29, 1902: "Every one who by faith obeys God's commandments will reach the condition of sinlessness in which Adam lived before his transgression. When we submit ourselves to Christ, we live His life. This is what it means to be clothed with the garment of His righteousness."

COL 160: "None of the apostles or prophets ever claimed to be without sin. Men who have lived nearest to God, men who would sacrifice life itself rather than knowingly commit a wrong act, men whom God had honored with divine light and power, have confessed the sinfulness of their own nature. They have put no confidence in the flesh, have claimed no righteousness of their own, but have trusted wholly in the righteousness of Christ. So will it be with all who behold Christ."

AA 561-562: "Let not God be dishonored by the declaration from human lips: I am sinless; I am holy. Sanctified lips will never give utterance to such presumptous words."

DA 82: "But they could be saved through Christ only as by faith they should make His life their own."

9T 20: "Those who have been buried with Christ in baptism are to rise to newness of life, giving a living representation of the life of Christ."

(Letter from Basle, Switzerland, Dec. 8, 1886): "That which God required of Adam before his fall was perfect obedience to His law. God requires now what He required of Adam, perfect obedience, righteousness without a flaw, without shortcoming in His sight."

COL 57, 58: "At the very outset of the Christian life every believer should be taught its foundation principles. He should be taught that he is not merely to be saved by Christ's sacrifice, but that he is to make the life of Christ his life and the character of Christ his character."

RH Nov. 23, 1905: "When God's people bring the righteousness of Christ into the daily life, sinners will be converted, and victories over the enemy will be gained."

COL 69: "When the character of Christ shall be perfectly reproduced in His people, then He will come to claim them as His own."

COL 415: "At this time a message from God is to be proclaimed, a message illuminating in its influence and saving in its power. His character is to be known . . . The last rays of merciful light, the last message of mercy to be given to the world, is a revelation of His character of love."

GC 469: ". . . a character formed by obedience to that law will be holy. . . . The followers of Christ are to become like Him, — by the grace of God to form character in harmony with the principles of His holy law. This is Bible sanctification."

Proverbs 3:5, 6: "Trust in the Lord with all thine heart; and lean not unto thine own understanding."

DA 331: "Our lives may seem a tangle; but as we commit ourselves to the wise Master Worker, He will bring out the pattern of life and character that will be to His own glory. And that character which expresses the glory — character — of Christ will be received into the Paradise of God. A renovated race shall walk with Him in white, for they are worthy."

TM 499: "What is this glory? — The character of God."

CHRIST THE PATTERN MEDICAL MISSIONARY

Note: Jesus the pattern man **not only resisted evil but He devoted His life to doing good.** He revealed the loving, benevolent life of His Father.

MM 20: "Christ stands before us as the pattern Man, the great Medical Missionary, — an example for all who should come after. His love, pure and holy, blessed all who came within the sphere of its influence. His character was absolutely perfect, free from the slightest stain of sin. He came as an expression of the perfect love of God, not to crush, not to judge and condemn, but to heal every weak, defective character, to save men and women from Satan's power.

"What, then, is the example that we are to set to the world? We are to do the same work that the great Medical Missionary undertook in our behalf. We are to follow the path of self-sacrifice trodden by Christ.

"As I see so many claiming to be medical missionaries, the representation of what Christ was on this earth flashes before me. As I think of how far short the workers today fall when compared to the divine Example, my heart is bowed down with a sorrow that words cannot express. Will men and women ever do a work that bears the features and character of the great Medical Missionary?" . . .

Note: If we ministers must be purified and purged from our sins in order to make an offering in righteousness, must not this same preparation be made by our physicians and other medical workers?

DA 24: "As one of us, He gave an **example of obedience.** For this He took upon Himself our nature, and passed through our experiences. In all things it **behooved Him to be made like unto His**

74

brethren. If we had to bear anything which Jesus did not endure, then upon this point Satan would represent the power of God as insufficient for us. Therefore Jesus was 'in all points tempted like as we are.' He endured every trial to which we are subject. And **He exercised in His own behalf no power that is not freely offered to us. As man** He met temptation and overcame in the strength given Him from God."

Note: Let us remember that it was **not** the diety of the Son of God that was tempted, for God cannot be tempted with evil; but the **human** Christ was tempted as Adam and all men.

CONVERSION IS NOT COMPLETED UNTIL SIN IS DONE AWAY WITH AND CHARACTER IS PERFECTED

1 John 3:1-9: "We know that **when He shall appear, we shall be like Him; . . . And every man that hath this hope in Him purifieth himself even as He is pure."** . . .

"Whosoever is born of God doth not commit sin: for his seed remaineth in him; and he cannot sin, because he is born of God."

MH 180: "Christ came to make us partakers of the divine nature, and His word declares that humanity combined with divinity does not commit sin."

2T 505: "**None are living Christians** unless they are having a **daily experience** in the things of God, and **daily** practice self-denial, **cheerfully bearing** the cross and following Christ. Every living Christian will advance daily in the divine life. As he advances toward perfection, he experiences a **conversion to God every day; and this conversion is not completed until he attains to perfection** of Christian character, a full preparation for the finishing touch of immortality."

SC 74: "Consecrate yourselves to God in the morning; make this your very first work. Let your prayer be, 'Take me O Lord, as wholly Thine. I lay all my plans at Thy feet. Use me today in Thy service. Abide with me, and let all my work be wrought in Thee.' This is a daily matter. Each morning consecrate yourself to God for that day. Surrender all your plans to Him, to be carried out or given up as His providence shall indicate. Thus day by day you may be giving your life into the hands of God, and thus your life will be molded more and more after the life of Christ. A life in Christ is a life of restfulness. There may be no ecstasy of feeling, but there should be an abiding, peaceful trust."

2T 512: "This daily review of our acts, to see whether conscience approves or condēmns, is necessary for all who wish to arrive at the perfection of character."

9T 154: "God demands that the appetites be cleansed, and that self-denial be practiced in regard to those things which are not good. This is a work that will have to be done before His people can stand before Him a perfected people."

OHC 163 (L 9a, 1891): "When souls are converted, their salvation is not yet accomplished. They then have the race to run; the arduous struggle is before them to 'fight the good fight of faith . . . The battle is lifelong, and must be carried forward with determined energy proportionate to the value of the object you are in pursuit of, which is eternal life."

Ev 192 (RH Aug. 19, 1890): "Without the transforming process . . . the original propensities to sin are left in the heart."

AA 565: "We are not perfect; but it is our privilege to cut away from the entanglements of self and sin, and advance to perfection."

NBL Vol. 1, A Work of Cooperation, Education, No. 4, Vol. 1, No. 28: "We may all strive for perfection of character, but all who come into possession of it will earn it step by step, by the cultivation of the virtues which God commends."

BY CONSTANTLY BEHOLDING
WE ARE CHANGED

2 Cor. 3:18: "But we all, with open face beholding as in a glass the glory of the Lord, are changed into the same image from glory to glory even as by the Spirit of God."

TM 367: "No human being is righteous any longer than he has faith in God and maintains a vital connection with Him."

FILB 138 (MS 1, 1878): "The helpless sinner must cling to Christ as his only hope. If he lets go his hold for a moment, he imperils his own soul and the souls of others."

FILB 135 (RH Dec. 16, 1884): "The evil tendencies of mankind are hard to overcome. The battles are tedious. Every soul in the strife knows how severe, how bitter, are these contests. Everything about growth in grace is difficult, because the standard maxims of the world are constantly interposed between the soul and God's holy standard."

5T 47: "We must gain the victory over self, crucify the affections and lusts; and then begins the union of the soul with Christ . . . After this union is formed, it can be preserved only by continual, earnest, painstaking effort. Every Christian must stand on guard continually, watching every avenue of the soul, where Satan might find access. He must pray for divine help and at the same time resolutely resist every inclination to sin. By courage, by faith, by persevering toil, he can conquer. But let him remember that to gain the victory Christ must abide in him and he in Christ. . . . It is only by personal union with Christ, by communion with Him daily, hourly, that we can bear the fruits of the Holy Spirit."

FE 195: "Terrible are the consequences of not having a **constant** connection with God."

DA 71: "Jesus was placed where His character would be tested. **It was necessary for Him to be constantly on guard in order to preserve His purity.** He was subject to all the conflicts which we have to meet, that He might be an example for us in childhood, youth, and manhood."

2T 189: "The reason it is so difficult for men and women to live religious lives is because they do not exercise the mind unto godliness. It is trained to run in the opposite direction. Unless the mind is **constantly** exercised in obtaining spiritual knowledge, and in seeking to understand the mystery of godliness, it is incapable of appreciating eternal things, because it has no experience in that direction. This is the reason why nearly all consider it up-hill business to serve the Lord."

ST Sept. 12, 1892: "At times when we have exercised a little faith, we have experienced a little help, and we have hoped to be victorious overcomers. But have we had faith that through Christ we should be able to overcome every temptation **as He overcame?** We have **not generally exercised this quality of faith.**"

RH Jan. 24, 1893: "Some will not make a right use of the doctrine of justification by faith. They will present it in a **ONE-SIDED** manner, making everything of faith and belittling works. Others will seize the points that have a leaning toward error, and will ignore works altogether. Now genuine faith always works by love; it supplies a motive power. Faith is **not an opiate, but a stimulant.** . . . Looking to Calvary will not quiet your soul into non-performance of duty, but will create faith that will work, purifying the soul from all selfishness. In laying hold of Christ by faith, we but just begin our work. Every man has corrupt and sinful habits, that must be overcome through vigorous warfare. Every soul must fight the fight of faith."

EW 114: "The remnant are to overcome by the blood of the Lamb and the word of their testimony. Some expect to overcome alone by the blood of the Lamb, without making any special effort of their own."

SC 50: "The poor sufferer was helpless; he had not used his limbs for thirty-eight years. Yet Jesus bade him 'rise, take up thy bed, and walk.' The sick man might have said, 'Lord, if Thou wilt make me whole, I will obey Thy word.' But no, he believed Christ's word, believed that he was made whole, and he made the effort at once; he willed to walk, and he did walk. **He acted on the word of Christ, and God gave the power.** He was made whole."

KH 229 (ST June 16, 1890): "The faith we are required to have is not a do-nothing faith; saving faith is that which works by love and purifies the soul . . . Faith and works will keep us evenly balanced, and make us successful in the work of perfecting Christian character."

Rev. 14:12 "Here are they that keep the commandments of God and the faith of Jesus."

John 5:4 "For whatsoever is **born** of God overcometh the world: and this is the victory that overcometh the world, **even our faith.**"

Notebook Leaflet, Christian Experience No. 11, page 2: Letter 120, 1898: "Looking unto Jesus . . . I can overcome all things . . . saying the words in faith, "I am in Christ."

DA 679: "He, Jesus, knew that the life of His trusting disciples would be like His, a series of uninterrupted victories, not seen to be such here, but recognized as such in the great hereafter."

Sanctified Life 60: "But as we repent of our sins against God, and seek pardon through the merits of Christ, He will impart that faith which works by love and purifies the heart."

Steps to Christ 52: "Through this simple act of believing God, the Holy Spirit has begotten a new life in your heart."

GC 489: "He (Satan) is constantly seeking to deceive the followers of Christ with his fatal sophistry that it is impossible for them to overcome."

1T 144: "We can overcome, yes fully, entirely, Jesus died to make a way of escape for us that we might overcome every evil temper, every sin, every temptation, and sit down at last with Him."

WHAT ABOUT YOUR READING, TELEVISION, RADIO?

AA 518-519: "The apostle sought to teach the believers how important it is to keep the mind from wandering to forbidden themes, or from spending its energies on trifling subjects. Those who would not fall a prey to Satan's devices, must **guard well the avenues of the soul;** they must **avoid reading, seeing** or **hearing that which will suggest impure thoughts.** The mind must not be left to dwell at random upon every subject that the enemy of souls may suggest. The heart must be faithfully sentineled, or evils without will awaken evils within, and the soul will wander in darkness. 'Gird up the loins of your mind,' Peter wrote, 'be sober, and hope to the end for the grace that is to be brought unto you at the revelation of Jesus Christ; . . . not fashioning yourselves according to the former lusts in your ignorance: but as He which hath called you is holy, so be ye holy in all manner of conversation; because it is written, Be ye holy; for I am holy.' "

MYP 105 (YI Jan. 4, 1900): "Many of us fail to improve our privileges. We make a **few feeble efforts** to do right, and then go back to our old life of sin. If we ever enter the kingdom of God, we must enter with perfect characters, not having spot, or wrinkle, or any such thing."

FILB 114 (MS 48, 1893): "Christ came to the world to counteract Satan's falsehood that God had made a law which men could not keep. Taking humanity upon Himself, He came to this earth, and by a life of obedience showed that God has not made a law that man cannot keep. He showed that it is possible for man perfectly to obey the law. . . . Man is to show by his obedience that he could be trusted in heaven, that he would not rebel."

5T 472: ". . . We are to exert every energy of the soul in the work of overcoming, and to look to Jesus for strength to do what we cannot do of ourselves . . ."

GC 425 "Through the grace of God and their own diligent effort, they must be conquerors in the battle with evil. While the investigative judgment is going forward in heaven, while the sins of penitent believers are being removed from the sanctuary, there is to be a special work of purification, of putting away of sin, among God's people upon earth. This work is more clearly presented in the messages of Revelation 14."

OHC 218 (RH June 28, 1882): "Heaven may pour its choicest blessings upon him; he may have all possible assistance on the right hand and on the left; and yet all will be in vain, unless he shall put forth earnest effort to help himself. He himself must engage in the warfare against sin and Satan, or he will fail of everlasting life."

8T 125: "I have a most earnest desire that you shall enter the City of God, not as a culprit barely pardoned, but as a conqueror."

AA 565: "We are not yet perfect; but it is our privilege to cut away from entanglements of self and sin and advance to perfection. Great possibilities, high and holy attainments are placed within the reach of all."

PERFECTION AT EVERY STAGE
OF DEVELOPMENT

COL 65: "The germination of the seed represents the beginning of spiritual life, and the development of the plant is a beautiful figure of Christian growth. As in nature, so in grace, there is no life without growth. The plant must either grow or die. As its growth is silent and imperceptible, but **continuous,** so is the development of Christian life. **At every stage of development our life may be perfect; yet if God's purpose for us is fulfilled, there will be continued advancement.**"

IHP 154 (RH Jan. 11, 1912): "The Lord gave an important lesson to His people in all ages when to Moses on the mount He gave instruction regarding the building of the tabernacle. In that work He required perfection in every detail . . . Into all to which the Christian sets his hand should be woven the thought of the life eternal. If the work performed is agricultural or mechanical in its nature, it may still be after the pattern of the heavenly . . ."

FILB 140 (L 9, 1899): "God requires moral perfection in all . . . Aim for perfection, and never, never lower the standard of righteousness to accommodate inherited and cultivated tendencies to wrong."

OHC 29 (L 25, 1882): ". . . the perfection of Christian character is to be the aim, the purpose of our life . . . **Like Christ** is the watchword . . . "

1 John 3:1-9: "We know that **when He shall appear, we shall be like Him; . . . And every man that hath this hope in Him purifieth himself even as He is pure.**" . . .

"Whatsoever is born of God doth not commit sin: for his seed remaineth in him; and he cannot sin, because he is born of God."
DA 671: "The honor of God and the honor of Christ is involved in the perfection of the character of His people."

THE APOSTLE PAUL'S CONSTANT
CONFLICT WITH SELF

8T 313: "**Paul's sanctification** was a result of a **constant conflict with self.** He said, 'I die daily.' His will and his desires every day conflicted with duty and the will of God. Instead of following inclination, he did God's will, however crucifying to his own nature.

"God leads His people on step by tep. **The Christian life is a battle and a march.** In this warfare there is no relief; the effort must be continuous and persevering. It is by unceasing endeavor that we maintain the victory** over the temptations of Satan. Christian .integrity must be sought with resistless energy, and maintained with a resolute fixedness of purpose.

"**No one will be borne upward without stern, persevering effort in his own behalf.** All must engage in this warfare

81

for themselves. **Individually** we are responsible for the issue of the struggle; **though Noah, Job, and Daniel** were in the land, they could deliver neither son nor daughter by their righteousness."

The Sanctified Life, 10: "There is no such thing as instantaneous sanctification. True sanctification is a daily work continuing as long as life shall last."

Ibid 94: "Sanctification is a progressive work."

Letter 155, 1902: "This sanctification is a progressive work, and an advance from one stage of perfection to another."

ST Feb. 17, 1904: "The work of sanctification begins in the home. Those who are Christians in the home will be Christians in the church and in the world. In the home the spirit of criticism and fault finding should have no place. The peace of the home is too sacred to be marred by this spirit . . . Restrain every hasty speech that struggles for utterance. Before you speak that fretful, impatient word, stop and think of the influence which, if spoken, it will exert."

CT 20: "But they can make advancement only through conflict . . . Appetite and passion must be brought under the control of the Holy Spirit. There is no end to the warfare this side of eternity."

Redemption, or the Teaching of Christ, Calvary, 82: ". . . Christ was the prince of sufferers; but it was not bodily anguish that filled Him with horror or dispair; it was a sense of the malignity of sin, a knowledge that man had become so familiar with sin that he did not realize its enormity, that it was so deeply rooted in the human heart as to be difficult to eradicate."

KH 88 (L 66, 1898): "The Lord requires us to sink self in Jesus Christ, and let the glory be all of God."

SC 43: "The warfare against self is the greatest battle that was ever fought."

5T 82: "There are few really consecrated men among us; few who have fought and conquered in the battle with self."

DA 118: "For our sake He exercjsed a self-control stronger than hunger or death. And in this first victory were involved other issues that enter into all our conflicts with the powers of darkness."

6T 626: "Those who abide in Jesus will be happy, cheerful and joyful in God. A subdued gentleness will mark the voice, reverance for spiritual and eternal things will be expressed in the actions, and music, joyful music will echo from the lips, for it is wafted from the throne of God. This is the mystery of godliness, not easily explained, nonetheless felt and enjoyed."

MYP 98 (YI Aug. 2, 1902): "Words cannot describe the peace and joy possessed by him who takes God at His word. Trials do not disturb him, slights do not vex him. Self is crucified."

KH 287 (RH Aug. 2, 1881): "The peace which passeth knowledge will cost us battles with the powers of darkness, struggles severe against selfishness and inward sins."

6 BC 1111 (MS 33, 1911): "The life of the Christian is not all smooth. He has stern conflicts to meet. Severe temptations assail him. 'The flesh lusteth against the Spirit, and the Spirit against the flesh.' The nearer we come to the close of this earth's history, the more delusive and ensnaring will be the attacks of the enemy. His attacks will grow fiercer and more frequent. Those who resist light and truth will become more hardened and unimpressible, and more bitter against those who love God and keep His commandments."

1SM 336 (ST Dec. 26, 1892): "But those who are waiting to behold a magical change in their characters without determined effort on their part to overcome such, will be disappointed."

EW 114: "The remnant are to overcome by the blood of the Lamb and the word of their testimony. Some expect to overcome alone by the blood of the Lamb, without making any special effort of their own."

PP 509: "Joshua had received the promise that God would surely overthrow these enemies of Israel, yet he put forth as earnest effort as though success depended upon the armies of Israel alone. He did all that human energy could do, and then he cried in faith for divine aid. The secret of success is the union of divine power with human effort."

PK 487: "His grace is given to work in us to will and to do, but never as a substitute for our effort."

RH June 11, 1901: "If we are faithful in **doing our part, in cooperating with Him,** God will work through us to do the good pleasure of His will, **but cannot work through us if we make no effort.** If we gain eternal life, we must work, and work earnestly. . . . **Our part is to put away sin, seek with determination for perfection of character. As we thus work, God cooperates with us.** . . . Let us not be deceived by the oft-repeated assertion, 'all we have to do is believe.' **Faith and works are two oars which we must use equally**

if we would press our way up the stream. . . . 'Faith, if it hath not works, is dead, being alone.' The Christian is a man of thought and practice. His faith fixes its roots firmly in Christ. **By faith** and **good works** he keeps his spirituality strong and healthy, and his spiritual strength increases **as he strives** to work the works of God."

A MESSAGE TO THE YOUNG

1T 158: "I saw that unless there is an entire change in the young, a thorough conversion, they may despair of heaven. . . . Many are leaning upon a supposed hope, without a true foundation. The fountain is not cleansed, therefore the streams proceeding from that fountain are not pure. Cleanse the fountain and the streams will be pure. If the heart is right, your **words,** your **dress,** your **acts,** will all be right. True godliness is lacking. I would not dishonor my Master so much as to admit that a careless, trifling, prayer-less person is a Christian. **No; a Christian has victory over his besetments, over his passions,** There is a remedy for the sin-sick soul. That remedy is in Jesus. Precious Saviour! His grace is sufficient for the weakest; and the strongest must also have His grace or perish.

"I saw how this grace could be obtained. **Go to your closet** and there alone plead with God; 'create in me a clean heart, O God, and renew a right spirit within me.' Be in earnest, be sincere. Fervent prayer availeth much. Jacob-like, wrestle in prayr. Agonize. Jesus in the garden, sweat great drops to blood; you must make an effort. **Do not leave your closet until you feel strong in God; then watch,** and just as long as you watch and pray, you can keep these evil besetments under, and the grace of God can and will appear in you."

2T 505: **"None are living Christians** unless they are having a **daily experience** in the things of God, and **daily** practice self-denial, **cheerfully bearing** the cross and following Christ. Every living Christian will advance daily in the divine life. As he advances toward perfection, he experiences a **conversion to God every day;** and **this conversion is not completed until he attains to perfection** of Christian character, a full preparation for the finishing touch of immortality."

84

RH Jan. 6, 1885: "However complete may have been our consecration at conversion it will avail us nothing unless it be renewed daily; but a consecration that embraces the actual present is fresh, genuine, and acceptable to God."

6T 400: "God's plan is first to get at the heart Speak the truth, and let Him carry forward the reformatory power and principle. Make no reference to what opponents say; but let the truth alone be advanced."

COL 337: "Under all circumstances . . . reproof should be spoken in love, then our words will reform and not exasperate."

6T 96: "Our appearance in every respect should be '. . . with modesty of demeanor . . .'"

Sanctuary.., Gulley (MS 153, 1899): "The Lord has given His holy commandments to be a wall of protection around His created beings, and those who will keep themselves from the defilement of appetite and passion may become partakers of the divine nature. Their perception will be clear."

GOD IS TESTING HIS PEOPLE

1T 187-188: **"Said the angel,** 'God will bring His work closer and closer **to test and prove very one of His people.'** Some are willing to receive one point; but when God brings them to **another testing point,** they shrink from it and stand back, because they find that it strikes directly at some **cherished idol.** Here they have opportunity to see what is in their hearts that shuts out Jesus. . . . Individuals are tested and proved a length of time to see if they will sacrifice their idols and heed the counsel of the True Witness. **If any will not be purified through obeying the truth, and overcome their selfishness, their pride, and evil passions,** the angels of God have the charge, 'they are joined to their idols, let them alone,' and they pass on to their work, leaving these with their sinful traits unsubdued, to the control of evil angels. **Those who come up to every point, and stand every test and overcome,** be the price what it may, have heeded the counsel of the True Witness, and they will receive the latter rain, and thus be fitted for translation."

5T 695: "Those who listened to the words of Christ, heard and reported His teaching just according to the spirit that was in them. It is ever thus with those who hear God's word. The manner in which they understand and receive it, depends upon the spirit which dwells in their hearts."

TM 79: "Satan takes control of every mind that is not decidedly under the control of the Spirit of God."

Eze. 14:1-6: ". . . that setteth up his idols in his heart . . . and cometh to the prophet; I the Lord will answer him that cometh according to the multitude of his idols; that I may take the house of Israel in their own hearts, because they are all estranged from Me through their idols."

MM 143 (MS 4a, 1885): "The intelligent soul . . . through the grace of Christ will say to the passions of the heart as he points to God's Moral Standard of righteousness, 'Hitherto shalt thou come and no further, and here shall thy proud waves be stayed; and the grace of Christ shall be as a wall of fire around about the soul.'"

4T 656: ". . . he who is mastered by his passions is a weak man. The real greatness and nobility of the man is measured by the power of the feelings he subdues, not by the power of the feelings that subdue him. The strongest man is he, who, while sensitive to abuse, will yet restrain passion and forgive his enemies. Such men are true heroes.

COL 270: "When the voice of God awakens the dead, he will come forth with the same appetites and passions, the same likes and dislikes that he cherished when living. **God works no miracle to re-create a man who would not be re-created when he was granted every opportunity and provided with every facility.**"

CDF 49: ". . . After man has done all in his power to ensure health, by the denying of appetite and gross passions that he may possess a healthy mind, and a sanctified imagination, that he may render to God an offering in righteousness, then he is saved alone by a miracle of God's mercy, as was the ark upon the stormy billows. Noah had done all that God required of him in making the ark secure; then God performed that which man could not do, and preserved the ark by His miraculous power."

RH Feb. 18, 1904: "I must overcome the temptations that surround me, else they will drive Christ from my heart. He combats all temptation and braves all opposition. By the strength obtained from on high, he holds in control the passions and tendencies which uncontrolled, would lead him to defeat."

Letter Oct. 10, 1899: "One little disregard of 'thus saith the Lord' is sufficient to stop the promised blessing of the Holy Spirit."

OHC 278 (RH Sept. 1, 1885): "Enoch's life and character, which was so holy that he was translated to heaven without seeing death, represents what the lives and charcters of all must be, if, like Enoch, they are to be translated when Christ shall come."

EW 283: "God would be honored by making a covenant with those who had kept His law in the sight of the heathen round about them; and Jesus would be honored by translating, without their seeing death, the faithful, waiting ones who had so long expected Him."

THE POWER OF THE HUMAN WILL

5T 513: "Pure religion has to do with the will. The will is the governing power in the nature of man, bringing all the other faculties under its sway. The will is not the taste or the inclination, but it is **the deciding power,** which works in the children of men unto obedience to God, or unto disobedience . . ."

CT 222: "Strength of character consists of two things — POWER OF THE WILL and POWER OF SELF-CONTROL."

COL 333: "As the will of man cooperates with the will of God it becomes omnipotent."

COL 331: "The impossibility lies in your own will. If you will not, then you cannot overcome."

5T 513: "You will be in constant peril until you understand the true force of the will. You may **believe and promise all things, but your promises or your faith are of no value until you put your will on the side of faith and action.** If you fight the fight of **faith with all your will-power, you will conquer. Your feelings, your impressions, your emotions, are not to be trusted, for they are not reliable . . ."**

MB 95: "It is through the will that sin retains its hold upon us. The **surrender of the will** is represented as plucking **out the eye** or cutting off the hand."

FILB 135 (RH Dec. 10, 1884): "The evil tendencies of mankind are hard to overcome. The battles are tedious. Every soul in the strife knows how severe, how bitter, are these contests. Everything about growth and grace is difficult, because the standard maxims of the world are constantly interposed between the soul and God's holy standard. . . . We must gain the victory over self, crucify the affections and lusts; and then begins the union of the soul with Christ . . . After this union is formed, it can be preserved only by continual, earnest, painstaking effort.

"Every Christian must stand on guard continually, watching every avenue of the soul, where Satan might find access. He must pray for divine help and at the same time resolutely resist every inclination to sin. By courage, by faith, by persevering toil, he can conquer. But let him remember that to gain the victory Christ must abide in him and he in Christ. . . . It is only by personal union with Christ, by communion with Him daily, hourly, that we can bear the fruits of the Holy Spirit."

MB 97: "God does not design that our will should be destroyed; for it is only through its exercise that we can accomplish what He would have us do. **Our will is to be yielded to Him, that we may receive it again, purified and refined, and so linked in sympathy with the Divine that He can pour through us the tides of His love and power.**"

Ed 289: "The will should be guided and moulded, but not ignored or crushed. Save the strength of the will; in the battle of life it is needed."

HL 232: "Keep the power of the will awake, for the will aroused and rightly directed is a potent soother of the nerves."

OHC 153 (RH Aug. 25, 1896): "When Satan is permitted to mold the will, he uses it to accomplish his ends . . . He stirs up the evil propensities, awakening unholy passions and ambitions. . . . the human will must be blended with the divine. This will bring the Holy Spirit to our aid."

TM 79: "Satan takes control of every mind that is not decidedly under the control of the Spirit of God."

MYP 55: "Our finite will must be brought into submission to the will of the Divine; the human will must be blended with the Divine. This will bring the Holy Spirit to our aid."

A Solemn Appeal, 29: "If Satan seeks to divert the mind from this to low and sensual things, bring it back again, and place it on eternal things; and when the Lord sees the determined effort made to retain only pure thoughts, He will attract the mind, like the magnet, and purify the thoughts, and enable them to cleanse themselves from every secret sin."

Sanctifed Life, 93: "**If the mind wanders,** we must **bring it back;** by persevering effort, habit wlll finally make it easy."

TM 240: "The Lord does not propose to perform for us either the willing or the doing. This is our proper work. As soon as we earnestly enter upon the work, God's grace is given to work in us to will and to do, but never as a substitute for our effort. Our souls are to be aroused to cooperate. The Holy Spirit works the human agent, to work out our own salvation. This is the practical lesson the Holy Spirit is striving to teach us."

RH June 26, 1900: "The apostles and prophets and holy men of old did not perfect their characters by a miracle. They used the ability given them by God trusting alone in the righteousness of Christ; and all who will use the same means may secure the same result . . . Here the false doctrine that man has nothing to do but believe is swept away. Eternal life is given to us on the condition that we obey the Commandments of God."

AA 482-483: "God wishes us to have the mastery over ourselves. . . . Of ourselves, we are not able to bring the purposes and desires and inclinations into harmony with the will of God; 'but if we are willing to be made willing,' the Saviour will accomplish this for us, 'casting down imaginations; and every high thing that exalteth itself against the knowledge of God, and bringing into captivity every thought to the obedience of Christl'"

Solemn Appeal, 49: "It is constant war against the carnal mind, aided by the refining influence of the grace of God, which will attract it upward, and habituate it to meditate upon pure and holy things."

GW 126: "By **watchfulness and prayer,** he may so **guard his weakest points** that they will become his **strongest points.**"

2 Peter 1:4: "Whereby are given unto us exceeding great and precious promises: that by these ye might be partakers of the divine nature, having escaped the corruption that is in the world through lust."

5T 148: "If you will only watch, continually watch unto prayer, if you will do everything as if you were in the immediate presence of God, you will be saved from yielding to temptation, and may hope to be kept pure, spotless, and undefiled to the last . . . If Christ be within us we shall crucify the flesh with the affections and lust."

OHC 216 (Lb 1891): " 'Watch unto prayer', and you will steadily grow in grace and in a knowledge of Christ . . . All unawares to yourself you will have expanded like the wide-spreading cedar, and many will profit by your counsel."

KH 209 (L 46, 1898): "Be determined that you will not become angry . . . that you will not be hasty and overbearing. If this is your weak point, guard that point as a man would guard a broken limb. Watch your spirit, and let not a hasty spirit conquer you."

WE MUST REFLECT THE IMAGE OF JESUS FULLY

EW 71: "I also saw that many do not realize what they must do in order to live in the sight of the Lord without a high priest in the sanctuary through the time of trouble. Those who receive the seal of the living God and are protected in the time of trouble **must reflect the image of Jesus fully.**

"I saw that many were neglecting the preparation so needful and were looking to the time of 'refreshing' and the 'latter rain' to fit them to stand in the day of the Lord and to live in His sight. Oh, how many I saw in the time of trouble without a shelter! They had neglected the needful preparation; therefore they could not receive the refreshing that all must have to fit them to live in the sight of a holy God. Those who refuse to be hewed by the prophets and fail to purify their souls in obeying the whole truth, and who are willing to believe that their condition is far better than it really is, will come **up to the time of the falling of the plagues,** and then see that they needed to be hewed and squared for the building. But there will be no time then to do it and no Mediator to plead their cause before the Father."

5T 214: "Not one of us will ever receive the seal of God while our characters have one spot or stain upon them."

RH June 6, 1902: "Are we striving with all our power to attain the stature of men and women in Christ? Are we seeking for His fullness ever pressing toward the mark set before us — the perfection of His character? When the Lord's people reach this mark they will be sealed in their foreheads. Filled with the spirit they will be complete in Christ, and the recording angel will declare, 'It is finished.' "

7BC 970 (RH May 21, 1895): "The seal of the living God will be placed upon those only who bear a likeness to Christ in character."

7BC 970 (ST July 18, 1911): "As wax takes the impression of the seal, so the soul is to take the impression of the Spirit of God and retain the image of Christ."

4BC 1161 (Ms 173, 1902): "Just as soon as the people of God are sealed in their foreheads — it is not any seal or mark that can be seen, but a settling into the truth, both intellectually and spiritually, so they cannot be moved — just as soon as God's people are sealed and prepared for the shaking, it will come. Indeed, it has begun already."

5T 216: "Now is the time to prepare. The seal of God will never be placed upon the forehead of an impure man or woman. It will never be placed upon the forehead of the ambitious, world-loving man or woman. It will never be placed upon the forehead of men or women of false tongues or deceitful hearts. All who receive the seal must be without spot before God — candidates for heaven."

RH Nov. 22, 1892: "If you would stand through the time of trouble, you must know Christ, and appropriate the gift of His righteousness, which He imputes to the repentant sinner."

MH 454: "By a life of holy endeavor and firm adherence to the right, the children of God are to seal their destiny."

RH Nov. 4, 1890: "No man can cover his soul with the garment of Christ's righteousness while practicing known sins, or neglecting known duties. God requires the entire surrender of the heart, before justification can take place; and in order for man to retain justification, there must be continual obedience, through active living faith that works by love and purifies the soul."

AA 54-55: ". . . Some . . . are idly waiting for some special season of spiritual refreshing . . . But unless the members of God's church today have a living connection with the source of all spiritual growth, they will not be ready for the time of reaping . . . instead of looking forward to some future time when, through a special endowment of spiritual power they will receive a miraculous fitting up for soul-winning, they are yielding themselves daily to God, that He may make them vessels meet for His use."

1SM 336 (ST Dec. 26, 1894): "Those who are waiting to behold a magical change in their character without determined effort on their part to overcome sin, will be disappointed."

TM 507: "They expect that the lack will be supplied by the latter rain . . . They are making a terrible mistake."

GC 620: "Those who delay a preparation for the day of God cannot obtain it in the time of trouble, or at any subsequent time. **The case of all such is hopeless.**"

1T 261: "I was shown God's people waiting for some change to take place, a compelling power to take hold of them. But they will be disappointed, for they are wrong. They must act, they must take hold of the work themselves and earnestly cry to God for a true knowledge of themselves."

EW 71: "I saw that none could share the 'refreshing' unless they obtain the victory over every besetment, over pride, selfishness, love of the world and over every wrong word and action. We should therefore, be drawing nearer and nearer to the Lord, and be earnestly seeking that preparation necssary to enable us to stand in the battle of the day of the Lord. Let all remember that God is holy and that none but holy beings can ever dwell in His presence."

1T 619: "I was shown that if God's people make no efforts on their part, but wait for the refreshing to come upon them and remove their wrongs and correct their errors; if they depend upon that to cleanse them from filthiness of the flesh and spirit, and fit them to engage in the loud cry of the third angel, they will be found wanting. The refreshing or power of God comes only on those who have prepared themselves for it by doing the work which God bids them, namely, cleansing themselves from all filthiness of the flesh and spirit, perfecting holiness in the fear of God."

2T 401-402: "A few, yes, only a few, of the vast number who people the earth will be saved unto life eternal, while the masses who have not perfected their souls in obeying the truth will be appointed to the second death."

THERE WILL BE THOSE WHO WILL MEET THIS REQUIREMENT. WILL YOU BE ONE OF THEM?

5T 476: "These are they that stand upon Mount Zion with the Lamb, having the Father's Name written in their foreheads. . . . In their mouth was found no guile; for they are without fault before the throne of God. Now is reached the complete fulfillment of those words of the angel: (Zech. 3:8) 'Hear now, Oh Joshua the high priest, thou, and thy fellows that sit before thee; for they are **men wondered at;** . . . Now indeed are the **remnant 'men wondered at,'** as the tears and humiliation of their pilgrimage give place to joy and honor in the presence of God and the Lamb."

TM 18: "The Lord Jesus is making experiments on human hearts through the exhibition of His mercy and abundant grace. He is effecting transformations so amazing that Satan, with all his triumphant boasting, with all his confederacy of evil united against God and the laws of His government, stands viewing them as a fortress impregnable to his sophistries and delusions. They are to him an incomprehensible mystery. The angels of God, seraphim and cherubim, the powers commissioned to cooperate with human agencies, look on with astonishment and joy, that fallen men, once children of wrath, are through the training of Christ, developing characters after the divine similitude, to be sons and daughters of God, to act an important part in the occupations and pleasures of heaven."

MY DECLARATION OF FAITH

God helping me, I will live up to the light I have and will seek more light by a faithful study of the Bible and the Spirit of Prophecy; claiming victory moment by moment, hour by hour, and day by day, until habit becomes character and victory is mine.

MS 159, 1898: "Practice often repeated, grows into confirmed habit and becomes character."

THE LOUD CRY AND TRANSLATION

RH Nov. 29, 1892: "The Saviour of men will be glorified and **the earth will be lightened with the bright beams of His righteousness."**

Ibid: "The loud cry of the third angel has already **begun** in the revelation of the righteousness of Christ, the sin-pardoning Redeemer. This is the **beginning** of the light of the angel whose glory shall fill the whole earth."

GCB April 3, 1901: Thirteen years after the Minneapolis meeting, at the General Conference of 1901, Sister White said: "I feel a special interest in the movements and decisions that shall be made at this Conference regarding the things that should have been done years ago, and especially ten years ago when we were assembled in Conference, and the Spirit and power of God came into our meeting, testifying that God was ready to work for this people if they would come into working order. **The brethren assented to the light God had given, but . . . the light that was given was not acted upon . . .** year after the same acknowledgment was made, but the principles which exalt a people were not woven into the work."

Note: Since the light of 1888 was the **beginning** of the light of the angel whose glory shall fill the whole earth, may not the light revealed in this study be the fulness of the light that is to perfect the characters necessary for translation? If so, has not the time come to fulfill this call of God?

RH April 1, 1890: "Several have written to me, inquiring if the message of justification by faith is the third angel's message, and I have answered, it is the third angel's message in verity."

RH Nov. 4, 1890: "No man can cover his soul with the garment of Christ's righteousness while practicing known sins, or neglecting known duties. God requires the entire surrender of the heart, before justification can take place; and in order for man to retain justification, there must be continual obedience, through active living faith that works by love and purifies the soul."

ST July 29, 1902: "Every one who by faith obeys God's commandments will reach the condition of sinlessness in which Adam lived before his transgression. When we submit ourselves to Christ, we live His life. This is what it means to be clothed with the garment of His righteousness."

6T 19: "The message of Christ's righteousness is to sound from one end of the earth to the other to prepare the way of the Lord. This is the glory of God which closes the work of the third angel."

TM 499: "What is this glory? — The character of God."

COL 415-416: "The last rays of merciful light, the last message of mercy to be given to the world, is a revelation of His character of love. The children of God are to manifest His glory. In their own life and character they are to reveal what the grace of God has done for them."

COL 333: "As the will of man cooperates with the will of God it becomes omnipotent."

RH Nov. 23, 1905: "When God's people bring the righteousness of Christ into the daily life, sinners will be converted, and victories over the enemy will be gained."

AA 54-55: ". . . Some . . . are idly waiting for some special season of spiritual refreshing. . . . But unless the members of God's church today have a living connection with the source of all spiritual growth, they will not be ready for the time of reaping . . . instead. of looking forward to some future time when, through a special endowment of spiritual power they will receive a miraculous fitting up for soul-winning, they are yielding themselves daily to God, that He may make them vessels meet for His use."

1SM 336 (ST Dec. 26, 1892): "Those who are waiting to behold a magical change in their character without determined effort on their part to overcome sin, will be disappointed."

TM 507: "They expect that the lack will be supplied by the latter rain . . . They are making a terrible mistake."

SL 84: "The prophets and apostles did not perfect Christian character by a miracle. They used the means which God had placed within their reach; and all who will put forth the same effort will secure the same results."

Isa. 60:1-3: "Arise, shine; for thy light is come, and the glory (character) of the Lord is risen upon thee. For, behold, the darkness shall cover the earth, and gross darkness the people: but the Lord shall arise upon thee, and His glory shall be seen upon thee.

"And the Gentiles shall come to thy light and kings to the brightness of thy rising."

THE SECRET OF MEETING EVERY DIFFICULTY, THE PRESCRIPTION FOR THE HEALING OF ALL MENTAL, PHYSICAL, AND SPIRITUAL ILLS

9T 124: " 'Come unto Me, all ye that labor and are heavy laden, and I will give you rest.' **THIS IS A PRESCRIPTION** FOR THE HEALING OF ALL MENTAL AND PHYSICAL AND SPIRITUAL ILLS. It is Christ's gift to those who seek Him in sincerity and in truth."

MH 71: "In these words, Christ was speaking to every human being. Whether they know it or not, all are weary and heavy laden. All are weighed down with burdens that only Christ can remove. . . . He will take the load from our weary shoulders. He will give us rest."

MH 249: ". . . He desires us to lay our perplexities and troubles at His feet, and **LEAVE THEM THERE.**"

7T 297: "Jesus consents to bear our burdens **ONLY** when we trust Him."

7T 274: "Pray in faith. And **be sure to bring your lives into harmony with your petitions,** that you may receive the blessings for which you pray. Let not your faith weaken; for the **blessings received are proportionate to the faith exercised.** 'According to your faith be it unto you.' "

OHC 313 (L9, 1873): "We do not always consider that the sanctification we so earnestly desire and for which we pray so earnestly is brought about through the truth and, by the providence of God, in a manner we least expect. When we look for joy, behold there is sorrow. When we expect peace, we frequently have distrust and doubt, because we find ourselves plunged into trials we cannot avoid. In these trials we are having the answers to our prayers. In order for us to be purified, the fire of affliction must kindle upon us, and our will must be brought into conformity to the will of God. . . . God sees it best to put us under a course of discipline which is essential for us before we are fit subjects for the blessing we crave . . . Perfection of Christian character can be attained only through labor, conflict, and self-denial. . . . He brings us into positions which are the most trying to reveal what is in our hearts. To further the development of Christian graces He will place us in circumstances which will demand increased exertion on our part to keep our faith in lively exercise."

2T 321: "Believing brings peace, and trusting in God brings joy."

3T 378: "You must then answer your own prayer as far as possible, by resisting temptation, and leave that which you cannot do for yourselves for Jesus to do for you."

TM 407: "The contest will wax more and more fierce on the part of Satan; for he is moved by a power from beneath. As the work of God's people moves forward with sanctified resistless energy, **planting the standard of Christ's righteousness in the church,** moved by a power from the throne of God, **the great controversy will wax stronger and stronger,** and will become more and more determined. **Mind will be arrayed against mind,** plans against plans, principles of heavenly origin against principles of Satan. Truth in its varied phases will be in conflict with error in its ever-varying increasing forms and which, if possible, will deceive the very elect."

6BC 1111 (MS 33, 1911): "The life of the Christian is not all smooth. He has stern conflicts to meet. Severe temptations assail him. 'The flesh lusteth against the Spirit, and the Spirit against the flesh.' The nearer we come to the close of this earth's history, the more delusive and ensnaring will be the attacks of the enemy. His attacks will grow fiercer and more frequent. Those who resist light and truth will become more hardened and unimpressible, and more bitter against those who love and keep His commandments."

GW 162: "Unless divine power is brought into the experience of the people of God, **false theories and ideas will take minds captive,** Christ and His righteousness will be dropped out of the experience of many, and their faith will be without power or life."

"Words of Caution." Aug. 27, 1903: "False theories will be mingled with every phase of experience and advocated with Satanic earnestness in order to captivate the mind of every soul who is not rooted and grounded in a full knowledge of the Sacred principles of the word. In the very midst of us will arise false teachers giving heed to seducing spirts whose doctrines are of satanic origin. These teachers will draw disciples after themselves, creeping in unawares, they will use flattering words, and make skillful misrepresentations with seductive tact."

RH Jan. 24, 1893: The servant of God gives us a warning against **Satan's attempt to confuse minds regarding the "right use of the doctrine of justification by faith. . . .** He (Satan) will work with his masterly power to bring in **fanaticism** on one hand and cold **formalism** on the other, **that he may gather in a harvest of souls.** Now is the time to watch unceasingly. Watch for the first steps of advance that Satan may make against us. There are dangers to be guarded against on the right hand and on the left. Some will not make a right use of the doctrine of justification by faith, they will present it in a **one-sided manner,** making everything of faith and belittling works."

Letter 68, 1894: "Fanaticism will appear in the very midst of us. Deception will come, and of such a character that if it were possible they would mislead the very elect. If marked inconsistencies and untruthful utterances were apparent in these manifestations, the words from the lips of the Great Teacher would not be needed. It is because of the many and varied dangers that would arise, that this warning is given.

"The reason why I hang out the danger signal is, that **through the enlightenment of the Holy Spirit of God I can see that which my brethren do not discern. . . .** It is enough for me to tell you, be on your guard; and as faithful sentinels keep the flock of God from accepting indiscriminately all that professes to be communicated to them from the Lord."

RH Nov. 4 1890: "No man can cover his soul with the garment of Christ's righteousness while practicing known sins, or neglecting known duties. God requires the entire surrender of the heart, before justification can take place; and in order for man to retain justification, there must be continual obedience, through active living faith that works by love and purifies the soul."

GW 301: "This I know, that our churches are dying for the want of teaching on the subject of righteousness by faith in Christ and on kindred truths."

GC 472: "The testimony of the word of God is against this ensnaring doctrine of faith without works. It is not faith that claims the favor of heaven without complying with the conditions upon which mercy is to be granted, it is presumption; for genuine faith has its foundation in the promise and provisions of the Scriptures."

2SM 381 (L 55, 1886): "I do not mean that cheap faith unsupported by works, but that earnest, living, constant, abiding faith, that eats the flesh and drinks the blood of the Son of God."

1SM 382 (ST June 16, 1890): "When it is in the heart to obey God, when efforts are put forth to this end, Jesus accepts this disposition and efforts as man's best service, and He makes up for the deficiency with His own divine merit. But He will not accept those who claim to have faith in Him, and yet are disloyal to His Father's commandment. We hear a great deal about faith, but we need to hear a great deal more about works. Many are deceiving their own souls by living an easygoing, accommodating, crossless religion. But Jesus says, 'If any man will come after me, let him deny himself, and take up his cross, and follow me.' "

PP 73: "Without the works of obedience, faith is 'dead'."

2SM 78: "The **very last deception of Satan will be to make of none effect the testimony of the Spirit of God** . . . Satan will work ingeniously in different ways, and through different agencies, to unsettle the confidence of God's remnant people in the true testimony."

Special Testimony, Sept. 8, 1898 (MS 113, 1898): "Man can accomplish nothing without God, and **God has arranged His plans so as to accomplish nothing in the restoration of the human race without the cooperation of the human with the divine.** The part man is required to sustain is **immeasurably small,** yet in the plan of God it is just that force that is needed to make the work a success. We are laborers together with God. This is the Lord's own wise arrangement. The cooperation of the human will and endeavor with divine energy **is the link** that binds men up with one another and with God."

RH Nov. 29, 1892: "The work of the Holy Spirit is **immeasurably great** . . . the personal presence of Christ in the soul."

1SM 42 (L 73, 1903): "The testimonies themselves will be the key that will explain the messages given, as scripture is explained by scripture." (Here a little and there a little. Isa. 28:10).

1SM 48 (L 40, 1890): "There will be a hatred kindled against the testimonies which is satanic. The workings of Satan will be to unsettle the faith of the churches in them, for this reason: Satan cannot have so clear a track to bring in his deceptions and bind up souls in his delusions if the warnings and reproofs and counsels of the Spirit of God are heeded — ."

1SM 47 (Ms 1, 1883): "Many a man professes to accept the testimonies, while they have no influence upon his character. His faults become stronger by indulgence until, having been often reproved and not heeding the reproof, he loses the power of self-control, and becomes hardened in a course of wrongdoing. If he is overworked, if weakness comes upon him, he has not moral power to rise above the infirmities of character which he did not overcome; they become his strongest points, and he is overborne by them."

AA 482: "The work of gaining salvation is one of co-partnership, a joint operation. There is to be cooperation between God and the repentant sinner. This is necessary for the formation of right principles in the character. Man is to make earnest efforts to overcome that which hinders him from attaining to perfection. But he is wholly dependent upon God for success. Human effort of itself is not sufficient. Without the aid of divine power, it avails nothing. God works and man works. Resistance of temptation must come from man, who must draw his power from God."

RH Nov. 22, 1892: "Man is privileged to connect with Christ, and then the divine and the human combine; and in this union the hope of man must rest alone; for it is as the Spirit of God touches the soul that the powers of the soul are quickened, and man becomes a new creature in Christ Jesus."

MM 12: "The sick are to be healed through the combined efforts of the human and the divine. Sin brings physical and spiritual disease and weakness, Christ has made it possible for us to free ourselves of this curse. The Lord promises by the medium of truth to renovate the soul. The Holy Spirit will make all who are willing to be educated, able to communicate that truth with power. It will renew every organ of the body, that God's servants may work acceptably and successfully. Vitality increases under the influence of the Spirit's action. Let us by this power lift ourselves into a higher, holier atmosphere, that we may do well our appointed work."

2SM 15 (L 43, 1890): "Human effort must combine with divine power that we may be able to accomplish the closing work for this time."

NBL. The Church, No. 5, 3: "Unless the Holy Spirit works upon the human heart at every step, we shall stumble and fall."

THE RELATION OF THE HOLY SPIRIT
TO HUMAN EFFORT

TM 518: "As fast as the soul resolves to act . . . the Holy Spirit gives . . . strength. . . . The Spirit is supplied to cooperate with the soul's resolve."

Letter, Oct. 10, 1899: "One little disregard of 'thus saith the Lord' is sufficient to stop the promised blessing of the Holy Spirit."

KH 16 (RH July 18, 1882): "The Holy Spirit must be constantly imparted to man, or he has no disposition to contend against the powers of darkness."

COL 57-58: "At the very outset of the Christian life every believer should be taught its foundation principles. He should be taught that he is not merely to be saved by Christ's sacrifice, but that he is to make the life of Christ his life and the character of Christ his character."

IHP 338 (RH May 11, 1906): "The latter rain will never refresh and invigorate the indolent, who do not use the powers God has given them."

IHP 218 (Ms 9, 1863): "Those who decide to be on the Lord's side, and have made up their minds understandingly, have commenced a good work. Yet the work has but just begun. They have just enlisted in the army. The conflicts and battles are before them."

IHP 99 (RH April 5, 1890): "If you are abiding in Christ, and Christ is in you, you cannot speak angry words."

COL 335: "A **character** formed according to the divine likeness is the **only treasure** that we **can take from this world to the next.**"

DA 415-416: "Peter could not keep silent. He laid hold upon his Master, as if to draw Him back from His impending doom, exclaiming, 'Be it far from Thee, Lord; this shall not be unto Thee.' " "Peter loved his Lord; but Jesus did not commend him for thus manifesting the desire to shield Him from suffering. Peter's words were not such as would be a help and solace to Jesus in the great trial before Him. They were not in harmony with God's purpose of grace toward a lost world, nor with the lesson of self-sacrifice that Jesus had come to teach by His own example. **Peter did not desire to see the cross in the work of Christ.**"

IHP 63 (MS 20, 1899): "He did not neglect the smallest, simplest duty, **perfection** marked all that He did."

IHP 64 (RH Mar. 31, 1904): "Beholding Christ for the purpose of becoming like Him, the seeker after truth sees the perfection of the principles of God's law, and he becomes dissatisfied with everything but perfection. . . . But he knows that with the Redeemer there is saving power that will gain for him the victory in the conflict. The Saviour will strengthen and help him as he comes pleading for grace and efficiency."

4T 86: "God brings His people near Him by close testing trials, by showing them their own weakness and inability, and by teaching them to lean upon Him as their only hope and safeguard. **Then His object is accomplished.** They are prepared to be used in every emergency, to fill important positions of trust, and to accomplish the grand purposes for which their powers were given them."

5T 745-746: "Just before us is the closing struggle of the great controversy, when, with 'all power and signs and lying wonders, and with all deceivableness of unrighteousness,' Satan is to work to misrepresent the character of God, that he may 'seduce, if it were possible, even the elect.' If there was ever a people in need of constantly increasing light from heaven, it is the people that, in this time of peril, God has called to be the depositories of His Holy Law, and to vindicate His character before the world."

2 Peter 3:14 "Wherefore, beloved, seeing that ye look for such things, be diligent that ye may be found of Him in peace, without spot, and blameless."

PP 64: "But Christ, after having redeemed man from the condemnation of the law, could impart divine power, to unite with human effort. Thus, by repentance toward God and faith in Christ, the fallen children of Adam might once more become 'sons of God'."

RH April 12, 1870: "Opportunity is now given you to improve and become perfect this side of the judgment."

5T 79: "The prevailing spirit of our time is that of infidelity and apostasy — a spirit of pretended illumination because of a knowledge of the truth, but in reality of the blindest presumption. There is a spirit of opposition to the plain Word of God, and to the testimony of His Spirit. There is a spirit of idolatrous exultation of mere human reason above the revealed wisdom of God.

"There are men **among us** in responsible positions who hold that the opinion of a few conceited philosophers, so-called, are more to be trusted than the truth of the Bible, or the Testimonies of the Holy Spirit. Such a faith as that of Paul, Peter, or John, is considered old-fashioned, and insufferable at the present day. It is pronounced absurd, mystical, and unworthy of an intelligent mind.

"God has shown me that these men are Hazaels to prove a scourge to our poeple. They are wise above what is written."

COL 311: "Christ in His humanity wrought out a perfect character, and this **character** He offers to impart to us."

We'd love to send you a catalog of titles we publish
or even hear your thoughts, reactions, criticism,
about things you did or didn't like about this
or any other book we publish.

Just contact us at:

www.TEACHServices.com
1-800/367-1844